DIVIDING THE HEAVENS

A Manual for Horoscope Wheel Calculations

⌘

Leonard Williams

©1991

Special Thanks To

The late Al H. Morrison, for the stimulus
Linda Curtiss, for the introduction to Al and needed encouragement
My Family, for the patience to hear "It's almost finished!" many dozens of times

Table of Contents

⌘

Introduction vii

PART ONE: THE BASIC CROSS: MIDHEAVEN AND ASCENDANT 1

   Definitions 3
   Calculation of Local Sidereal Time 7
      Examples 8
   Geocentric Latitude 11
      Finding Geographic Latitude 12
      Calculating Geocentric Latitude 13
      Table of Geocentric Latitudes 15
   Midheaven Longitude Calculation 17
      Summary of MC Longitude Calculations 20
   Ascendant Longitude Calculation 21
      Summary of Asc Longitude Calculations 31
   Arctic Region Asc Calculations 33
      Asc Calculations for Lat $\geq$ (90° - OE) 35
      Special Cases 38
   Southern Hemisphere Ascendants 41
      Summary of Southern Hemisphere Asc Calculations 41
   Antarctic Ascendant Calculations 47
      Asc Calculations for South Latitude $\geq$ (90° - OE) 47
   Examples 51
   Appendix to Part One 57
      Rectification of Birth Time From a Proven Ascendant 59
      Examples 62

PART TWO: FURTHER DIVISIONS: THE TWELVE HOUSES 65

   Introduction 67
PORPHYRY AND ALCABITIUS 69
   Introduction 71
   Porphyry 73
      Examples 75
   Alcabitius 81
      Examples 87

CAMPANUS AND REGIOMONTANUS 93
Introduction 95
Campanus 97
Campanus at Circumpolar Latitudes 105
Examples 111
Regiomontanus 117
Regiomontanus at Circumpolar Latitudes 123
Examples 129
KOCH 135
Koch 137
Examples 149

Diagrams and Models 155

Introduction

Several years ago I was advised by Al H. Morrison, friend and mentor, that in spite of my penchant for precision in horoscope calculations *sans* computer, many of my charts would bear inaccuracies because of my reliance on a single old table of houses. You see, my Dalton's **Table of Houses** was erected on the mean obliquity of the ecliptic of 1885 (23° 27' 15"), but that angle is constantly changing with the precession and nutation of the earth's polar axis. It is currently 23° 26' 21". Well, he was right, but I wasn't quite sure I wanted to go out and buy several tables of houses computed for different OE's (sometimes not even specified) to cover birth dates from various decades of this century; however, the seeds of doubt had been sown.

The remedy? Find a text on astrological computations that doesn't refer one to a table of houses? No such luck: the computer programmers must have them all! So, to refresh my memory of mathematical fields too long left fallow, I borrowed a trigonometry text from the library; twenty-five dollars bought me a solar powered scientific calculator (with necessary trig functions); the ever-changing obliquity of the ecliptic (a very impressive phrase to have at tongue-tip) I can find for any month in my **American Ephemeris** by Michelsen. Add to that many months of head scratching.

The results? I found it is not at all difficult to calculate precisely the Midheaven and Ascendant longitudes for any time, latitude and OE. Double interpolations from a table of houses are not, in fact, much simpler. Herein are the appropriate equations and their derivations for use by those who, like myself, desire accurate horoscope charting with minimal dependence on the computer programmer technocracy.

⌘

A note on method:

It is not my expectation that every reader of this manual be literate in trigonometry. To help interested persons get a handle on the process involved in this work, I have provided step by step derivations of final equations. (Many skeptics of astrology would probably be surprised at just how solid a legitimate technical basis there is for establishment of the parameters used in the interpretive art of astrology.) Following each section I have included a summary of derived equations for easier reference.

Some readers who are better versed in trigonometry may find a seeming inconsistency in my use of various trig identities to simplify equations. I have tried to make final equations as simple as possible while avoiding negative angles and ambiguous function values which may not be clearly sorted by a scientific calculator.

If you are using a scientific calculator for the first time, get familiar with its operations sequences: given a string of numbers and functions, which operations take precedence? For example, with a number entered and waiting, I can press "×", enter an angle in °/'/", convert that to decimal degrees, and find a trig function for it, before the actual multiplication of the waiting figure is carried out by the pressing of "=". If your calculator performs in a decimal degree mode, it is important to make the necessary conversions from °/'/", otherwise something like 12° 30' will be taken as 12.3° and not as the intended 12.5°.

PART ONE

THE BASIC CROSS:

MIDHEAVEN AND ASCENDANT

Definitions

Definitions may seem terribly rudimentary, but they do allow better mutual understanding of basic elements of any subject. The technical terms below are elements of the co-ordinate systems employed by astrology in the dividing up of the celestial sphere into angles and houses. These terms are as often misunderstood as understood, so I offer explanations to be on the safe side.

This list is not in the usual alphabetical order, but in order of the complexity and interdependence of the definitions.

Zenith: the point directly overhead, on a line from the earth's center through the event location to the celestial sphere. Opposite it is the **Nadir**.

Great Circle: The circle formed by the intersection of a sphere and a plane passing through its center.

Horizon: a great circle composed of all points 90° away from the zenith (or nadir). Its center is the earth's center. Full name is Rational Horizon, in distinction to the Apparent, or Visible, Horizon.

Meridian: a great circle passing through both zenith and nadir, crossing the horizon at right angles at north and south. The north and south poles of the earth are included in its sweep also. Usually the south side, or branch, of this circle is referred to as "the Meridian" (of a location).

Prime Vertical: a great circle intersecting the horizon at east and west, and the meridian at zenith and nadir. These intersections form right angles.

Equator (Celestial): the great circle created by projection of the earth's equator onto the celestial sphere. It intersects both horizon and prime vertical at east and west.

East Point: the point of intersection of the horizon, prime vertical and equator in the east.

Ecliptic: the great circle traced by the sun in its apparent annual trek around the celestial sphere. It intersects with the equator at ♈ and ♎, or 0° and 180° respectively, the equinoctial points.

Midheaven (MC, Medium Coeli): the point of intersection of the meridian and ecliptic, given in degrees of zodiacal longitude. Opposite it is the **Imum Coeli** (IC, Pit of the Heavens).

Ascendant: the point of intersection of the horizon and ecliptic in the east, given in degrees of zodiacal longitude.

Obliquity of the Ecliptic: the tilt of the earth's plane of rotation, or its axis of rotation, to the plane of its orbit around the sun. The angle varies periodically and by a predictable amount because of precession and nutation of the earth's axis; that is, the earth wobbles slightly like an unbalanced top because of the sun's and moon's unequal gravitational influences on it (lunisolar precession). The obliquity (OE) is seen on the celestial sphere as the angle between the equator and the ecliptic at their intersections at ♈ and ♎.

Pertinent co-ordinate measurements (Figure 1):

Right Ascension (RA): This is known to most astrologers as Sidereal Time (ST) and it is usually noted in hours/ minutes/ seconds. RA parallels the equator, running eastward, or counter-clockwise (clockwise in the southern hemisphere), and beginning with $0^h\,00^m\,00^s$ at the vernal equinoctial point, ♈. There are twenty-four hours of RA. Sidereal Time specifically refers to the RA crossing the meridian at a given time, giving an indication of the orientation of the earth with regard to the celestial sphere at that time and place. The hrs/ mins/ secs can be converted to degrees/ minutes/ seconds of arc at a rate of 15°/hr, 15'/min and 15"/sec.

Declination: degrees north or south of the equator and at right angles to it. The extent of declination is from 0° at the equator to 90° north or south, at the poles. The sun's declination varies seasonally from about 23.5° north in summer to about 23.5° south in winter. The extremes of the sun's declination equal the obliquity of the ecliptic.

Longitude (Celestial): also known as zodiacal or ecliptic longitude, this measurement in degrees runs eastward, or counter-clockwise (clockwise in the southern hemisphere), parallel to the ecliptic. RA equals longitude at four points only: 0°/♈, 90°/♋, 180°/♎ and 270°/♑.

Latitude (Celestial or Ecliptic): degrees north or south of the ecliptic and at right angles to it. Measurement is from 0° on the ecliptic to 90° north or south, at the poles of the earth's orbital plane. The sun's latitude is always 0°, since it always lies on the ecliptic.

Geocentric Latitude: (see Figure 2) measures degrees north or south of the equator, and at right angles to it, on the surface of the earth. It corresponds exactly to the celestial co-ordinates of declination, being measured in angles contiguous with the earth's center. Like declination, geocentric latitude runs from 0° on the equator to 90° at the poles. It can be measured on the celestial sphere as the angle between equator and prime vertical at the East Point, or, along the meridian, as the arc from equator to zenith.

Geo*centric* latitude is not to be confused with geo*graphic* latitude. The latter is measured in terms of the angle formed between a perpendicular, or normal, to the earth's surface, and the equator. Since the earth is ellipsoidal rather than spherical (exaggerated in Figure 2), these angles are not congruent with those of geo*centric* latitude, and the two systems of geodetic latitude coincide at only two places: the poles and the equator. Geographic latitude is not truly compatible with celestial co-ordinate systems used in astrological work.

Co-latitude: the trigonometric complement of geocentric latitude; *i.e.*, 90° minus (-) geocentric latitude. It can be measured on the celestial sphere as the angle between the horizon and the equator at the East Point, or, along the meridian as the arc from horizon to equator.

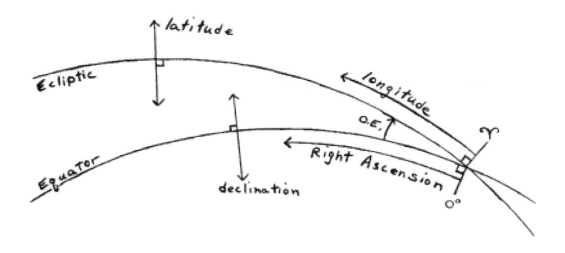

Figure 1

* * * * *

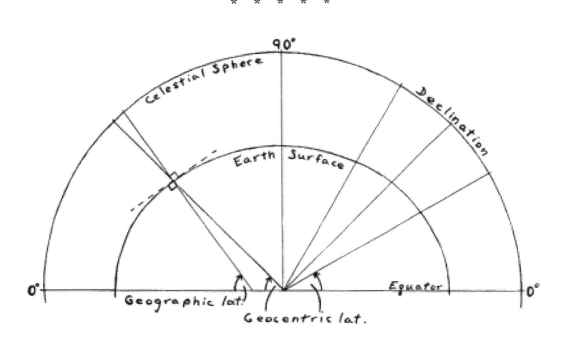

Figure 2

* * * * *

Note: All diagrams are of sections of the celestial sphere viewed from earth. For the southern hemisphere, Figures 1, 3 and 4 require mirror image reversal and replacement of signs with their opposites.

Other measurements used in this work:

Oblique Ascension: that point of the celestial equator crossing the horizon simultaneously with a given body or point in space. The Oblique Ascension of the Asc is coincident with the East Point, and is equal to the Right Ascension of the East Point.

Ascensional Difference: the difference between the right ascension and the oblique ascension of a body or point as seen from a given geocentric latitude.

Calculation of Local Sidereal Time

Sidereal Time is a celestial measurement along the celestial equator in hours, minutes and seconds. $0^h 00^m 00^s$ marks the Vernal Equinox, and the sidereal hours progress to the east to $23^h 59^m 59^s$ ST. Local Sidereal Time (LST) is the hour angle of the local meridian at a given time; LST thus is an indicator of the orientation of the earth's surface with regard to the heavens.

I. Data required for the calculation: birth (or event) time; birth longitude; an ephemeris

II. Definition of terms
SMT: Standard Mean Time, or clock time (less daylight additions)
SLD: Standard Longitude Difference, time zones. Time zones west of Greenwich are positive (+), zones east of Greenwich are negative (-).
LLD: Local Longitude Difference, the birth longitude divided by 15°/hr to convert °/'/" to h/m/s.
Longitude west of Greenwich is positive (+); longitude east of Greenwich is negative (-).
GMT: Greenwich Mean Time (or Universal Time).
GST: Greenwich Sidereal Time
GSTeph: Greenwich ST entered in the ephemeris for GMT 0^h or GMT 12^h of each day. Use the first entry prior to the standard time of birth.

III. Preparing data
A. Convert birth longitude to LLD by dividing it by 15°/hr.
B. For midnight ephemeris users: convert birth time to 24^h clock notation (standard, no daylight!). The birth time is incorporated into the calculation as SMT, a measure of mean time elapsed between the time of the ephemeris entry and the birth time.
C. For noon ephemeris users: as noted in (B), SMT is used as a measure of elapsed mean time from the ephemeris entry. In a 12^h ephemeris, this entry may likely be from the previous day. Make the following adjustments to the birth time to use it as SMT:

1) AM birth time: add 12 hours to birth time. Use GSTeph of previous day.

2) PM birth time: use conventional 12 hour clock notation, with GSTeph of same day.

D. Conversion of time units from h/m/s to decimal fractions of hours makes calculations considerably easier.

IV. Calculation

$$LST = [(SMT + SLD) \times (1.0027384 \text{ sid hr/ mean hr})] + GSTeph - LLD$$

Note: If bracketed portion plus GSTeph is less than LLD, increase the former by 24 hours. If the calculated LST exceeds 24 hours, simply subtract 24 hours from it.

❧ Examples ❦

1) March 5, 1951, 11:15 AM EST; longitude = 74.283333° W; GSTeph (0^h) = $10^h 47^m 44^s$

$SMT = 11.25^h$; $SLD = 5^h$; $GSTeph = 10.795556^h$;

$LLD = 4.9522222^h$

$LST = [11.25h + 5h) \times (1.0027384 \text{ sid hr/ mean hr})] +$
10.795556h - 4.9522222h

$LST = 22.137833^h$, or $22^h 08^m 16^s$

Using the same data with a noon ephemeris:

$SMT = 23.25^h$; GSTeph (from noon on March 4) = 22.762778^h

$LST = [(23.25h + 5h) \times (1.0027384 \text{ sid hr/ mean hr})] +$
22.762778h - 4.9522222h

$LST = 46.137916^h = 22.137916^h$, or $22^h 08^m 16^s$

2) May 20, 1979, 3:50 PM EDT; longitude = 76.141667° W; GSTeph (0^h) = 15.803611^h

$SMT = 14.83333^h$; $SLD = 5^h$; $LLD = 5.0761111^h$

$LST = [(14.83333h + 5h) \times 1.0027384 \text{ sid hr/ mean hr})] +$
15.803611h - 5.0761111h

$LST = 30.615141^h = 6.615141^h$, or $6^h 36^m 55^s$

Using the same data with a noon ephemeris:

$SMT = 2.83333^h$; GSTeph (from noon on May 20) = 3.8366667^h

$LST = [(2.83333h + 5h) \times (1.0027384 \text{ sid hr/ mean hr})] +$
3.8366667h - 5.0761111h

$LST = 6.6153364^h$, or $6^h 36^m 55^s$

❧ Additional Notes ❧

The bracketed portion of the equation converts elapsed standard mean hours to sidereal hours elapsed at Greenwich between the ephemeris entry time (0^h or 12^h) and the birth time. Adding GSTeph gives the GST of the birth time. LLD then serves to "relocate" from Greenwich to the local meridian.

Additional information about time and its computations can be found in astronomy handbooks such as Donald Menzel's **Field Guide to the Stars and Planets** (1964), which was helpful in the compilation of this material.

Ephemeris data used in the above calculations were from Neil Michelsen's **American Ephemeris for the Twentieth Century** (midnight); and the **Simplified Scientific Ephemeris** of the Rosicrucian Fellowship (noon).

Geocentric Latitude

Latitude and longitude are the two co-ordinates we use to register a locality on the earth's surface. Since the equatorial cross-section of the earth is circular, the divisions running around its circumference, the degrees of longitude, are regular and are measured by one system only. We need only distinguish between celestial and geodetic longitude, two quite different measurements.

In its longitudinal cross-section (through the poles), the earth is ellipsoidal, a characteristic exaggerated in Figure 2 (page 5). Subsequently, two different systems for measuring geodetic latitude have arisen. Perhaps the more commonly used of the two is *geographic* latitude. The measurement is of an angle formed between the equator and a perpendicular (or, more precisely, a normal) to the surface of the earth at the given locality. As a result of the earth's asphericity, the angles in question are not contiguous with the center of the planet. For measurements related strictly to the earth's surface, this system has proven to be quite adequate, and it is easily utilized with a plumb line or spirit level and a known celestial reference, such as the pole star or the sun (the latter with known declination for a given date).

The second system of measuring geodetic latitude is geo*centric*. The reference lines used are not established at the aspherical surface of the earth, but originate at the center of the earth, the intersection of the axis and the equatorial plane. Angles of geocentric latitude are, therefore, contiguous with the planet's center. While this system is not too readily employed in the field, being somewhat abstract, it is very compatible with celestial measurements used by astronomers and astrologers alike. Geocentric latitude is, in fact, congruent with declination, the north-south parameter in the celestial equatorial co-ordinate system. The slight wobble of the earth's axis caused by precession and nutation introduce a deviation between declination and geocentric latitude of no more than $\pm 0.54"$ or $\pm 0.009'$.

The direct relationship between geocentric latitude and celestial equatorial measurement make it an obvious choice over geographic latitude in astrology. Use of the latter system in the astrological work of relating the celestial sphere to a point on the earth's surface is a clear case of the classic mathematical taboo of adding apples to bananas.

So much for the what and why of geocentric latitude--the how remains to be demonstrated. Geocentric latitude is not generally found on maps, as are the parallels of geographic latitude. However, its calculation is simple, and, for those who don't mind interpolation, the table below converts each whole degree of geographic latitude to its geocentric counterpart. The derivation of the equation for conversion is included for those who, like myself, need to know how these things work.

The first step in converting geographic to geocentric latitude is to find, naturally, the former. At this point I would like to remind readers of the GIGO (Garbage-In--Garbage-Out) effect. While it is nice to have at one's disposal a method for obtaining a correct latitude measure, one's initial datum of geographic latitude should also be accurate. I would like, therefore, to take a little space to review a method for obtaining reasonably accurate geographic latitude that does not entail direct observation at the event locality in question.

❧ Finding Geographic Latitude ❦

Find a detailed area map for the locality; one is usually available for use at a library. Large scale topographics are among the best, especially for locating out-of-the-way places, like small hamlets or villages. The larger the scale, the better, but longitude and latitude must be included on the map. Using a millimeter rule or micrometer calipers, measure the distance from the parallel of latitude south of the locality to the parallel north of it. Next, measure the distance from the southern parallel up to the locality. Divide the latter distance by the distance between the parallels. Multiply the resulting fraction times the number of minutes of latitude between the two parallels used. Add the result to the southern parallel to obtain the actual geographic latitude of the locality. (Should the map include a scale relating linear distances to minutes of latitude, this task is greatly simplified.)

Example: On a particular map it is 25mm from 35° N 00' to 35° N 30'. It is 7.5mm from the 35° parallel up to Podonk Holler.

(7.5mm ÷ 25mm) × 30' = 9.0' north of the 35° parallel

Geographic latitude of the Holler is 35° N 09'

(This same technique can be used for locating the exact geodetic longitude, or the meridian, of a locality.)

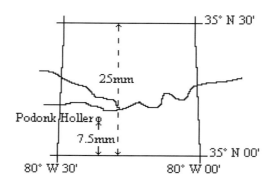

Calculating Geocentric Latitude

The earth is roughly an ellipsoid with polar radius of 6356.912 km and equatorial radius of 6378.388 km. The earth's elliptical cross-section plotted as points on Cartesian co-ordinates is defined by the equation

$$\frac{x^2}{a^2} + \frac{y^2}{b^2} = 1$$

where "a" is the equatorial radius and "b" is the polar radius.

Geographic latitude will be defined as the arctangent of the slope of the normal to any point (x,y) on the ellipse; geocentric latitude will be defined as the arctangent of y/x at the same point (x,y).

The equation as noted above must undergo numerous manipulations in order to make the desired latitude conversions:

$$y = b\sqrt{1 - \frac{x^2}{a^2}}$$

The tangent line at any point is the first derivative of the above:

$$m_t = \frac{-bx}{a^2 \sqrt{1 - \frac{x^2}{a^2}}}$$

The normal to any point is given by the negative reciprocal of the last equation:

$$m_n = \frac{a^2 \sqrt{1 - \frac{x^2}{a^2}}}{bx}$$

Since m_n, the trigonometric tangent of the geographic latitude, will be a known quantity, we should solve for x in terms of m_n:

$$x = a^2 \sqrt{\frac{1}{(m_n^2 \times b^2) + a^2}}$$

Substituting this identity for x into the second equation above, we have y in terms of m_n also:

$$y = b\sqrt{1 - \frac{a^2}{(m_n^2 \times b^2) + a^2}}$$

What we need to find is the tangent of the geocentric latitude, defined previously as y/x. So, with more substitutions and simplifications, we arrive at

$$\frac{y}{x} = m_n \times \frac{b^2}{a^2}$$

or

$$\tan \theta_c = \frac{b^2}{a^2} \times \tan \theta_g$$

where θ_c is the desired geocentric latitude and θ_g is the known geographic latitude. b^2/a^2, the ratio of the squares of the polar and equatorial radii, is a constant equal to 0.9932774. The equation for latitude conversion can be expressed finally as

$$\tan \theta_c = 0.9932774 \times \tan \theta_g$$

or

$$\text{geocentric lat} = \arctan[0.9932774 \times \tan(\text{geographic lat})]$$

Note that the geocentric latitude will always be less than the geographic latitude, but not by more than 11.6' (11' 36").

Table of Geocentric Latitudes

geocentric lat = arctan [0.9932774 × tan (geographic lat)]

θ_g = geographic latitude

θ_c = corresponding geocentric latitude

$\theta_g - \theta_c$ = amount of correction (-)

θ_g	θ_c	$\theta_g - \theta_c$	θ_g	θ_c	$\theta_g - \theta_c$
0°	0° 00' 00"	00' 00"	45°	44° 48' 24"	11' 36"
1°	0° 59' 36"	00' 24"	46°	45° 48' 25"	11' 35"
2°	1° 59' 12"	00' 48"	47°	46° 48' 26"	11' 34"
3°	2° 58' 48"	01' 12"	48°	47° 48' 28"	11' 32"
4°	3° 58' 24"	01' 36"	49°	48° 48' 31"	11' 30"
5°	4° 58' 00"	02' 00"	50°	49° 48' 35"	11' 25"
6°	5° 57' 36"	02' 24"	51°	50° 48' 39"	11' 21"
7°	6° 57' 12"	02' 48"	52°	51° 48' 44"	11' 16"
8°	7° 56' 49"	03' 11"	53°	52° 48' 51"	11' 09"
9°	8° 56' 26"	03' 34"	54°	53° 48' 58"	11' 02"
10°	9° 56' 03"	03' 57"	55°	54° 49' 06"	10' 54"
11°	10° 55' 40"	04' 20"	56°	55° 49' 14"	10' 46"
12°	11° 55' 18"	04' 42"	57°	56° 49' 24"	10' 36"
13°	12° 54' 56"	05' 04"	58°	57° 49' 34"	10' 26"
14°	13° 54' 34"	05' 26"	59°	58° 49' 45"	10' 15"
15°	14° 54' 13"	05' 47"	60°	59° 49' 57"	10' 03"
16°	15° 53' 52"	06' 08"	61°	60° 50' 09"	09' 51"
17°	16° 53' 32"	06' 28"	62°	61° 50' 22"	09' 38"
18°	17° 53' 12"	06' 48"	63°	62° 50' 36"	09' 24"
19°	18° 52' 53"	07' 07"	64°	63° 50' 51"	09' 09"
20°	19° 52' 34"	07' 26"	65°	64° 51' 06"	08' 54"
21°	20° 52' 16"	07' 44"	66°	65° 51' 22"	08' 38"
22°	21° 51' 58"	08' 02"	67°	66° 51' 38"	08' 22"
23°	22° 51' 41"	08' 19"	68°	67° 51' 56"	08' 04"
24°	23° 51' 24"	08' 36"	69°	68° 52' 13"	07' 47"
25°	24° 51' 08"	08' 52"	70°	69° 52' 32"	07' 28"
26°	25° 50' 53"	09' 07"	71°	70° 52' 51"	07' 09"
27°	26° 50' 38"	09' 22"	72°	71° 53' 10"	06' 50"
28°	27° 50' 24"	09' 36"	73°	72° 53' 30"	06' 30"
29°	28° 50' 01"	09' 49"	74°	73° 53' 50"	06' 10"
30°	29° 49' 59"	10' 01"	75°	74° 54' 11"	05' 49"
31°	30° 49' 47"	10' 13"	76°	75° 54' 32"	05' 28"
32°	31° 49' 36"	10' 24"	77°	76° 54' 54"	05' 06"
33°	32° 49' 25"	10' 35"	78°	77° 55' 16"	04' 44"
34°	33° 49' 16"	10' 44"	79°	78° 55' 39"	04' 21"
35°	34° 49' 07"	10' 56"	80°	79° 56' 01"	03' 59"
36°	35° 48' 59"	11' 01"	81°	80° 56' 24"	03' 36"
37°	36° 48' 52"	11' 08"	82°	81° 56' 48"	03' 12"
38°	37° 48' 46"	11' 14"	83°	82° 57' 11"	02' 49"
39°	38° 48' 40"	11' 20"	84°	83° 57' 35"	02' 25"
40°	39° 48' 35"	11' 25"	85°	84° 57' 59"	02' 01"
41°	40° 48' 31"	11' 29"	86°	85° 58' 23"	01' 37"
42°	41° 48' 28"	11' 32"	87°	86° 58' 47"	01' 13"
43°	42° 48' 26"	11' 34"	88°	87° 59' 11"	00' 49"
44°	43° 48' 25"	11' 35"	89°	88° 59' 36"	00' 24"
45°	44° 48' 24"	11' 36"	90°	90° 00' 00"	00' 00"

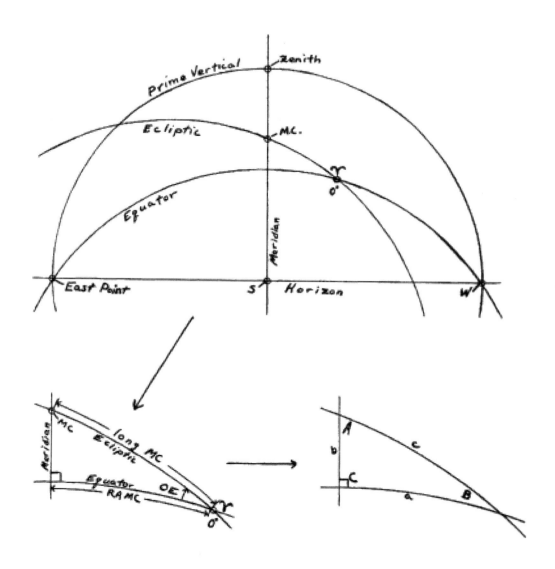

Figure 3

Midheaven Longitude Calculation

Calculation of the Midheaven (MC) longitude is derived from basic spherical trigonometric laws. Given an angle (OE) and one side (RAMC) of a right spherical triangle, one solves for a second side (MC longitude). The diagrams provided for reference are each in three parts: 1) a "wide angle" view of a section of the celestial sphere; 2) a more detailed drawing of the area under scrutiny; and 3) a standard trigonometric layout of the latter. In keeping with conventions of trigonometry, upper case letters represent angles, while lower case letters represent sides, or arcs, opposite angles of the same letter; *e.g.,* arc b is opposite angle B in triangle ABC.

The OE for a given event time can be found in an ephemeris or nautical almanac.

The abbreviation "lat" always refers to *geocentric,* not celestial, latitude. "MC" refers to Midheaven longitude.

I. Find Right Ascension of the MC (RAMC)

RAMC = Sidereal Time

This equation is simple enough, but for compatibility with other units of measurement used throughout these computations, the usual time units of ST and RA must be converted to degrees of arc. This operation is rather simple, with the conversion based on a rate of 15°/hr, 15'/min, and 15"/sec.

Example: ST = $12^h\ 30^m\ 30^s$

$$
\begin{aligned}
12^h \times 15°/h &= \qquad\qquad 180°\ 00'\ 00" \\
+ 30^m \times 15'/\text{min} &= 450' = \ \ 7°\ 30'\ 00" \\
+ 30^s \times 15"/\text{sec} &= 450" = \underline{\ \ 0°\ 07'\ 30"} \\
\text{ST} = \text{RAMC} &= 187°\ 37'\ 30"
\end{aligned}
$$

II. Find MC Longitude

Calculations of MC longitude fall into four categories established by the quadrant of the equator in which the RAMC lies.

    A.   For RAMC between 0° and 90° (Figure 3, facing page)
           RAMC = a, OE = B, and MC = c

In a right spherical triangle,

$$\tan c = \frac{\tan a}{\cos B}$$

Substituting,
$$\tan(MC) = \frac{\tan(RAMC)}{\cos(OE)}$$

B.   For RAMC between 90° and 180° (Figure 4)

OE = A, (180° - RAMC) = b, (180° - MC) = c, (RAMC - 90°) = x, and (MC - 90°) = y

In a right spherical triangle,
$$\cos A = \frac{\tan b}{\tan c}$$

Note that (b + x) = 90°: x is the complement of b. Similarly, y is the complement of c. Therefore
$$\tan b = \frac{1}{\tan x}$$
$$\tan c = \frac{1}{\tan y}$$

Substituting these identities,
$$\cos A = \frac{\tan y}{\tan x}$$

Rearranging, we get
$$\tan y = \cos A \times \tan x$$

Substituting again,
$$\tan(MC - 90°) = \cos(OE) \times \tan(RAMC - 90°)$$

C.   For RAMC between 180° and 270° (Figure 3, noting that in this quadrant the equator lies north of the ecliptic)

(RAMC - 180°) = a, OE = B, and (MC - 180°) = c

Using the same procedure as in Part A, we arrive at

$$\tan(MC - 180°) = \frac{\tan(RAMC - 180°)}{\cos(OE)}$$

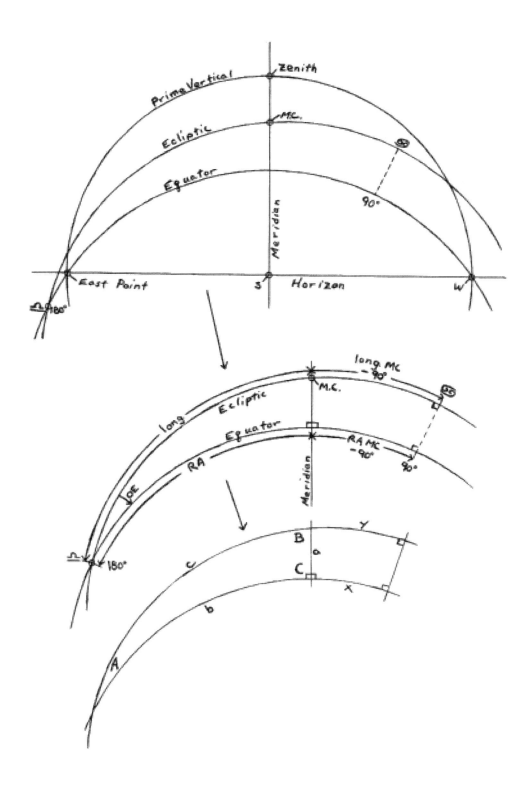

Figure 4

D. For RAMC between 270° and 360°/0° (Figure 4, noting that in this quadrant the equator lies north of the ecliptic)

OE = A, (360° - RAMC) = b, (360° - MC) = c, (RAMC - 270°) = x, and (MC - 270°) = y

Using the same procedure as in Part B, we obtain

tan (MC - 270°) = cos (OE) × tan (RAMC - 270°)

≈ Summary of MC Longitude Calculations ≈

I. Convert ST h/m/s to °/'/"

RAMC = ST

II. Calculate MC longitude

A. 0° ≤ RAMC < 90°

$$MC = \arctan\left[\frac{\tan(RAMC)}{\cos(OE)}\right]$$

B. 90° ≤ RAMC < 180°

MC = 90° + arctan [cos (OE) × tan (RAMC - 90°)]

C. 180° ≤ RAMC < 270°

$$MC = 180° + \arctan\left[\frac{\tan(RAMC - 180°)}{\cos(OE)}\right]$$

D. 270° ≤ RAMC < 360°/0°

MC = 270° + arctan [cos (OE) × tan (RAMC - 270°)]

Note: These equations are for use in either northern or southern hemisphere calculations.

Ascendant Longitude Calculation

In finding the Asc longitude one is seldom working with a right spherical triangle; consequently, more must be known for the solution of the triangle involved.

The "knowns" are two angles: geocentric latitude and OE; and one side: the Right Ascension of the East Point (RAEP). The latter arc is found by

$$RAEP = RAMC + 90°$$

During the course of equation derivations, the angle of geocentric latitude is most often used in finding an angle of (90° - lat), which is the co-latitude, or an angle of (90° + lat).

A second side of the triangle must be found, the Asc longitude arc. One is allowed by law (trigonometric law, that is) to solve for this arc by one of two methods. First, the desired arc may be found using the angle opposite to it, and a known side and its opposite angle. Secondly, one may use two known sides and their included angle (which is the angle opposite the desired side). Unfortunately, neither of these options fits our tally of knowns and unknowns in a directly usable way. So, we must find one other angle, which will be called "A", formed by the intersection of ecliptic and horizon.

Diagrams for this section are in three parts, as for the previous section. Equation derivations fall into four categories defined by the quadrant in which the RAEP is located.

The abbreviation "Asc" refers to Ascendant longitude, and "lat" refers to geocentric latitude.

I. For RAEP between 0° and 90° (Figure 5)

   RAEP = a, OE = B, (lat + 90°) = C, and Asc = c

   A. Find A

   In an oblique spherical triangle,

   $$\cos A = -\cos B \times \cos C + \sin B \times \sin C \times \cos a$$

   Substituting our knowns,

   $$\cos A = -\cos(OE) \times \cos(lat + 90°) + \sin(OE) \times \sin(lat + 90°) \times \cos(RAEP)$$

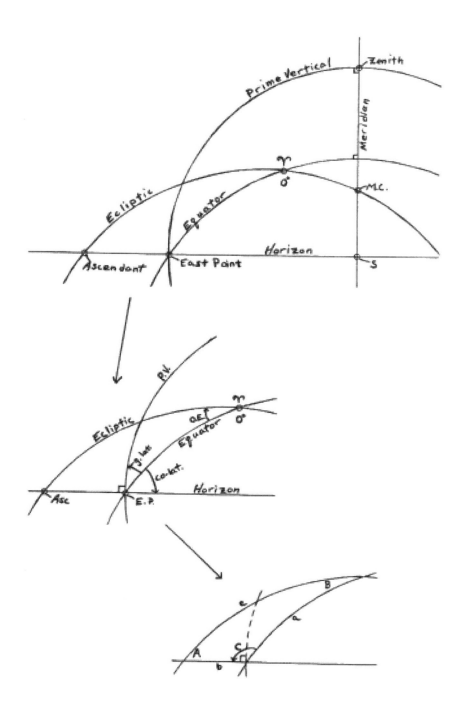

Figure 5

To simplify somewhat, note that

$$\sin(\text{lat} + 90°) = \cos(\text{lat})$$
$$\cos(\text{lat} + 90°) = -\sin(\text{lat})$$

Substituting again,

$$\cos A = -\cos(OE) \times [-\sin(\text{lat})] +$$
$$\sin(OE) \times \cos(\text{lat}) \times \cos(RAEP)$$

And finally

$$\cos A = \cos(OE) \times \sin(\text{lat}) +$$
$$\sin(OE) \times \cos(\text{lat}) \times \cos(RAEP)$$

B. Find Asc longitude

For this portion of derivation, a difficulty arises in this quadrant and one other. There is an ambiguous character to the sine and cosine values in the neighborhoods of 90° and 270° which can result in the mistaken calculation of the supplement of an angle rather than the angle itself. *E.g.*, sin 88° = sin 92° = .9993908. If the problem is not adequately resolved, an Ascendant which ought to be 92° (2° ♋) will be calculated to be 88° (28° ♊).

In order to avoid errors in this area, it is helpful first to calculate what the RAEP is when the Ascendant is exactly 90° at a given latitude. Through the miracle of polar equivalent triangles, we are able to convert our hypothetical triangle with two known angles (latitude and OE) and known side of 90° arc (Asc longitude) into a spherical right triangle with two known sides. Solving for one of the two remaining angles also solves for the supplement of the RAEP of our hypothetical triangle. Knowing at what RAEP the Ascendant longitude will pass the 90° mark allows us to compute without ambiguity any Asc in this quadrant by tailoring our equations to meet different situations.

The Critical RAEP (CRAEP) is found thus:

$$\cos(CRAEP) = \tan(OE) \times \tan(\text{lat})$$

To proceed: in an oblique spherical triangle,

$$\frac{\sin A}{\sin a} = \frac{\sin C}{\sin c}$$

Rearranging,

$$\sin c = \frac{\sin C \times \sin a}{\sin A}$$

Substituting,

$$\sin(\text{Asc}) = \frac{\sin(\text{lat} + 90°) \times \sin(\text{RAEP})}{\sin A}$$

Finally, with $\sin(\text{lat} + 90°) = \cos(\text{lat})$,

$$\sin(\text{Asc}) = \frac{\cos(\text{lat}) \times \sin(\text{RAEP})}{\sin A}$$

Here we make use of the CRAEP to tailor the general equation to particular situations:

1) RAEP < CRAEP

$$\text{Asc} = \arcsin\left[\frac{\cos(\text{lat}) \times \sin(\text{RAEP})}{\sin A}\right]$$

2) RAEP = CRAEP

   Asc = 90°

3) RAEP > CRAEP

$$\text{Asc} = 180° - \arcsin\left[\frac{\cos(\text{lat}) \times \sin(\text{RAEP})}{\sin A}\right]$$

II. For RAEP between 90° and 180° (Figure 6)

(180° - RAEP) = a, (180°- Asc) = b, colat = B, OE = C, (RAEP - 90°) = x, and (Asc - 90°) = y

A. Find A

Substituting into the law of cosines stated in Part I, we begin with

$$\cos A = -\cos(\text{colat}) \times \cos(\text{OE}) +$$
$$\sin(\text{colat}) \times \sin(\text{OE}) \times \cos(180° - \text{RAEP})$$

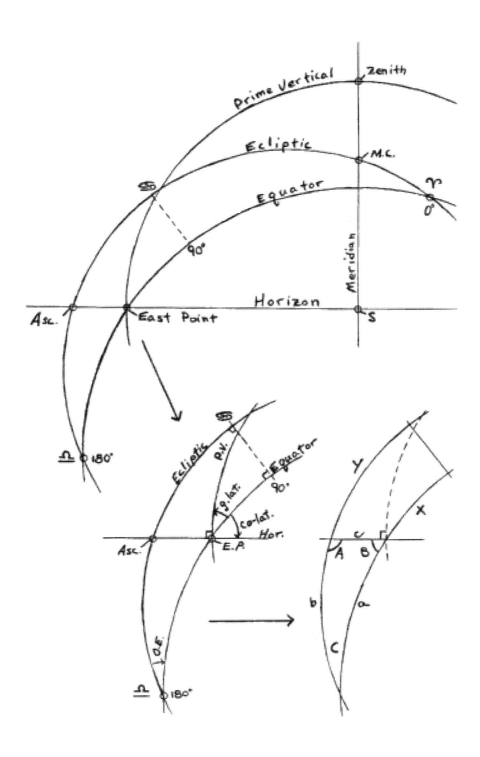

Figure 6

Latitude and co-latitude being complements,

$$\cos(\text{colat}) = \sin(\text{lat})$$
$$\sin(\text{colat}) = \cos(\text{lat})$$

Also

$$\cos(180° - \text{RAEP}) = -\cos(\text{RAEP})$$

These substitutions yield

$$\cos A = -\sin(\text{lat}) \times \cos(\text{OE}) +$$
$$\cos(\text{lat}) \times \sin(\text{OE}) \times [-\cos(\text{RAEP})]$$

A final rearrangement yields

$$\cos A = -\cos(\text{OE}) \times \sin(\text{lat}) -$$
$$\sin(\text{OE}) \times \cos(\text{lat}) \times \cos(\text{RAEP})$$

B.   Find Asc longitude

From the law of sines,

$$\frac{\sin A}{\sin a} = \frac{\sin B}{\sin b}$$

Thus

$$\sin b = \frac{\sin B \times \sin a}{\sin A}$$

Arc pairs a and x, b and y; and colat (angle B) and lat (90° - B) being complementary,

$$\sin a = \cos x$$
$$\sin b = \cos y$$
$$\sin B = \cos(90° - B)$$

An initial substitution gives us

$$\cos y = \frac{\cos(90° - B) \times \cos x}{\sin A}$$

Further substitution results in

$$\cos(\text{Asc} - 90°) = \frac{\cos(\text{lat}) \times \cos(\text{RAEP} - 90°)}{\sin A}$$

In this quadrant no special tailoring of the equation is necessary; no ambiguity is encountered.

III. For RAEP between 180° and 270° (Figure 7)

(RAEP - 180°) = a, (Asc - 180°) = b, colat = B, and OE = C

A. Find A

Substituting into the law of sines previously stated, begin with

$$\cos A = -\cos(\text{colat}) \times \cos(\text{OE}) + \sin(\text{colat}) \times \sin(\text{OE}) \times \cos(\text{RAEP} - 180°)$$

As in Part II, note that

$$\cos(\text{colat}) = \sin(\text{lat})$$
$$\sin(\text{colat}) = \cos(\text{lat})$$
$$\cos(\text{RAEP} - 180°) = -\cos(\text{RAEP})$$

Substitution and rearrangement yield

$$\cos A = -\cos(\text{OE}) \times \sin(\text{lat}) - \sin(\text{OE}) \times \cos(\text{lat}) \times \cos(\text{RAEP})$$

B. Find Asc longitude

From the law of sines we know that

$$\sin b = \frac{\sin B \times \sin a}{\sin A}$$

Accordingly,

$$\sin(\text{Asc} - 180°) = \frac{\sin(\text{colat}) \times \sin(\text{RAEP} - 180°)}{\sin A}$$

And finally

$$\sin(\text{Asc} - 180°) = \frac{\cos(\text{lat}) \times \sin(\text{RAEP} - 180°)}{\sin A}$$

Again, there are no ambiguities to circumvent in this quadrant.

IV. For RAEP between 270° and 360°/0° (Figure 8)

(360° - RAEP) = a, OE = B, (360° - Asc) = c, (lat + 90°) = C, (RAEP - 270°) = x, and (Asc - 270°) = y

A. Find A

Adapting the law of cosines to our variables, as in Part I, we have

$$\cos A = -\cos(\text{OE}) \times \cos(\text{lat} + 90°) + \sin(\text{OE}) \times \sin(\text{lat} + 90°) \times \cos(360° - \text{RAEP})$$

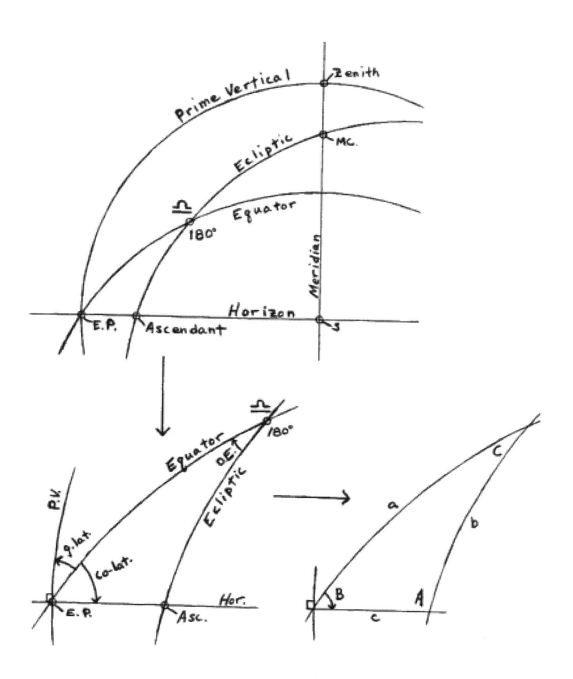

Figure 7

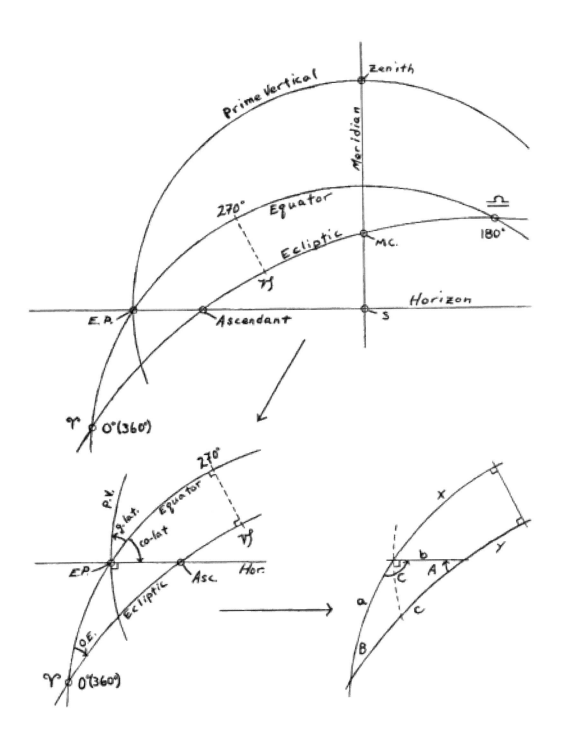

Figure 8

Noting once again that

$$\cos(\text{lat} + 90°) = -\sin(\text{lat})$$
$$\sin(\text{lat} + 90°) = \cos(\text{lat})$$
$$\cos(360° - \text{RAEP}) = \cos(\text{RAEP})$$

we can make substitutions that yield

$$\cos A = \cos(\text{OE}) \times \sin(\text{lat}) + \sin(\text{OE}) \times \cos(\text{lat}) \times \cos(\text{RAEP})$$

B. Find Asc longitude

The law of sines gives us

$$\sin c = \frac{\sin C \times \sin a}{\sin A}$$

Arc pairs a and x, c and y being complementary, we know that

$$\sin a = \cos x$$
$$\sin c = \cos y$$

Also, as noted above

$$\sin C = \sin(\text{lat} + 90°) = \cos(\text{lat})$$

Making the appropriate substitutions,

$$\cos y = \frac{\cos(\text{lat}) \times \cos x}{\sin A}$$

Final substitutions give

$$\cos(\text{Asc} - 270°) = \frac{\cos(\text{lat}) \times \cos(\text{RAEP} - 270°)}{\sin A}$$

This quadrant, however, requires the same special attention that the first quadrant did. A CRAEP must be calculated for the point at which the Ascendant longitude becomes 270°. A side trip into the realm of polar equivalent triangles allows us to formulate that for this quadrant and a given latitude.

$$\text{CRAEP} = 360° - \arccos[\tan(\text{OE}) \times \tan(\text{lat})]$$

Putting this information to use:

1) RAEP < CRAEP

$$\text{Asc} = 270° - \arccos\left[\frac{\cos(\text{lat}) \times \cos(\text{RAEP} - 270°)}{\sin A}\right]$$

2) RAEP = CRAEP

   Asc = 270°

3) RAEP > CRAEP

$$\text{Asc} = 270° + \arccos\left[\frac{\cos(\text{lat}) \times \cos(\text{RAEP} - 270°)}{\sin A}\right]$$

❧ *Summary of Asc Longitude Calculations* ❧

I. $0° \leq \text{RAEP} < 90°$

    A. A = arccos [cos(OE) × sin (lat) +

        sin (OE) × cos (lat) × cos (RAEP)]

    B. CRAEP = arccos [tan (OE) × tan (lat)]

    C. 1) RAEP < CRAEP

$$\text{Asc} = \arcsin\left[\frac{\cos(\text{lat}) \times \sin(\text{RAEP})}{\sin A}\right]$$

        2) RAEP = CRAEP

            Asc = 90°

        3) RAEP > CRAEP

$$\text{Asc} = 180° - \arcsin\left[\frac{\cos(\text{lat}) \times \sin(\text{RAEP})}{\sin A}\right]$$

II. $90° \leq \text{RAEP} < 180°$

    A. $A = \arccos[-\cos(OE) \times \sin(lat) - \sin(OE) \times \cos(lat) \times \cos(RAEP)]$

    B. $\text{Asc} = 90° + \arccos\left[\dfrac{\cos(lat) \times \cos(RAEP - 90°)}{\sin A}\right]$

III. $180° \leq \text{RAEP} < 270°$

    A. $A = \arccos[-\cos(OE) \times \sin(lat) - \sin(OE) \times \cos(lat) \times \cos(RAEP)]$

    B. $\text{Asc} = 180° + \arcsin\left[\dfrac{\cos(lat) \times \sin(RAEP - 180°)}{\sin A}\right]$

IV. $270° \leq \text{RAEP} < 360°/0°$

    A. $A = \arccos[\cos(OE) \times \sin(lat) + \sin(OE) \times \cos(lat) \times \cos(RAEP)]$

    B. $\text{CRAEP} = 360° - \arccos[\tan(OE) \times \tan(lat)]$

    C.   1) RAEP < CRAEP

$$\text{Asc} = 270° - \arccos\left[\dfrac{\cos(lat) \times \cos(RAEP - 270°)}{\sin A}\right]$$

        2) RAEP = CRAEP

$$\text{Asc} = 270°$$

        3) RAEP > CRAEP

$$\text{Asc} = 270° + \arccos\left[\dfrac{\cos(lat) \times \cos(RAEP - 270°)}{\sin A}\right]$$

Arctic Region Asc Calculations

Polar regions are herein defined by latitudes greater than the complement of the OE at any given time. This means, of course, that for the purpose of classifying sequences of calculations, the Arctic Circle must be viewed as shifting regularly with the OE.

Most people are familiar with the concept of periods of sunless days in the Arctic and Antarctic. At such times the sun's diurnal arc falls below the horizon. That portion of the ecliptic actually passes below the horizon daily whether the sun is there or not. It is the fact that this occurs to the south that poses the difficulty, since the ecliptic has this negative altitude only to the north at other latitudes. This must be accounted for in calculation of the Ascendant longitude.

The place to begin is in finding the boundaries of this "twilight zone". For a given latitude greater than (90° - OE), at what sidereal times (RAMC's) does the ecliptic cross the horizon at the Meridian? Consider the horizon projected onto the celestial sphere to the south, a great circle accompanying the ecliptic and equator (Figure 9). At the Meridian, the declination of the horizon will be found by

$$decl_h = lat - 90°$$

The negative result indicates south declination. The sidereal time span during which the ecliptic crosses the horizon to the south will be when the ecliptic has south declination also: between 180° and 360° of RA. The exact boundaries of the twilight zone will fall where the ecliptic has south declination equal to that of the horizon. Since we are deriving our final equations from measurements in RA (RAMC and RAEP), these boundaries, or twilight zone nodes, if you will, should be noted in RA.

Let the declination of the horizon be taken as (90° - lat), rather than as above, to avoid a negative angle. Then, from laws pertaining to right spherical triangles, we have

$$RA = 180° + \arcsin\left[\frac{\tan(decl_h)}{\tan(OE)}\right]$$

and

$$RA = 360° - \arcsin\left[\frac{\tan(decl_h)}{\tan(OE)}\right]$$

I will hereafter refer to these nodes as *Points of Critical Ecliptic Declination*, or PCED1 and PCED2. Between the two lies the twilight zone, centered on 270°, with its need for specially tailored Asc calculations.

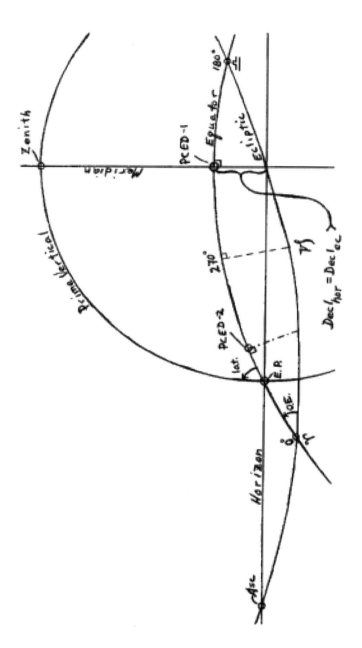

Figure 9

The basic equations for Asc longitude calculations in the north polar regions are derived from the same laws and same methods as previous Asc equations have been. One particular difference is that in the twilight zone derivations, (180° - OE) is used in place of the OE, much as the co-latitude was used instead of latitude in deriving previous equations. This is seen in angle B of Figures 10 and 11.

Note that at these latitudes a CRAEP is undefined. When in doubt about an Asc placement, make drawings and models. (See the end notes on this topic.)

Asc Calculations for Lat ≥ (90° - OE)

I. Find RAEP = RAMC + 90°

II. Find PCED's

    A. $Decl_h = 90° - lat$

    B. PCED calculation

        1) $PCED1 = 180° + \arcsin\left[\dfrac{\tan(decl_h)}{\tan(OE)}\right]$

        2) $PCED2 = 360° - \arcsin\left[\dfrac{\tan(decl_h)}{\tan(OE)}\right]$

III. Asc with PCED1 ≤ RAMC ≤ PCED2 (twilight zone)

    A. $A = \arccos[\cos(OE) \times \sin(lat) + \sin(OE) \times \cos(lat) \times \cos(RAEP)]$

    B. Asc longitude

        1) PCED1 ≤ RAMC < 270° (Figure 10)

$$Asc = \arcsin\left[\dfrac{-\cos(lat) \times \sin(RAEP)}{\sin A}\right]$$

        2) RAMC = 270°

           Asc = 0°

        3) 270° < RAMC ≤ PCED2 (Figure 11)

$$Asc = 360° - \arcsin\left[\dfrac{\cos(lat) \times \sin(RAEP)}{\sin A}\right]$$

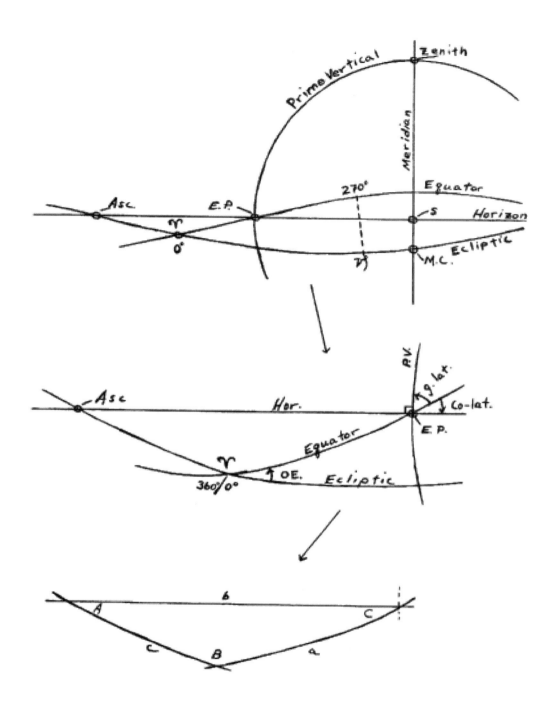

Figure 10

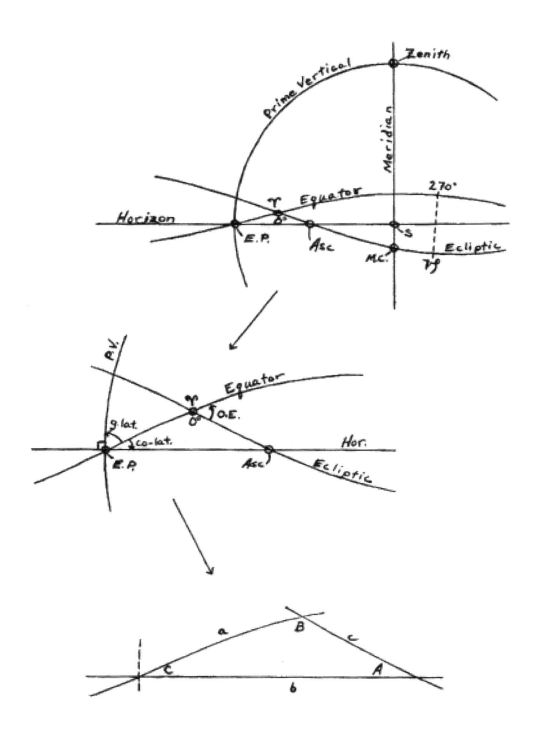

Figure 11

IV. Asc with RAMC outside twilight zone

A. $0° \leq RAEP < 90°$, $RAMC > PCED2$

1) $A = \arccos[\cos(OE) \times \sin(lat) + \sin(OE) \times \cos(lat) \times \cos(RAEP)]$

2) $Asc = 180° - \arcsin\left[\dfrac{\cos(lat) \times \sin(RAEP)}{\sin A}\right]$

B. $90° \leq RAEP < 180°$

1) $A = \arccos[-\cos(OE) \times \sin(lat) - \sin(OE) \times \cos(lat) \times \cos(RAEP)]$

2) $Asc = 90° + \arccos\left[\dfrac{\cos(lat) \times \cos(RAEP - 90°)}{\sin A}\right]$

C. $180° \leq RAEP < 270°$

1) $A = \arccos[-\cos(OE) \times \sin(lat) - \sin(OE) \times \cos(lat) \times \cos(RAEP)]$

2) $Asc = 180° + \arcsin\left[\dfrac{\cos(lat) \times \sin(RAEP - 180°)}{\sin A}\right]$

D. $270° \leq RAEP < 360°/0°$, $RAMC < PCED1$

1) $A = \arccos[(\cos(OE) \times \sin(lat) + \sin(OE) \times \cos(lat) \times \cos(RAEP)]$

2) $Asc = 270° - \arccos\left[\dfrac{\cos(lat) \times \cos(RAEP - 270°)}{\sin A}\right]$

❧ *Special Cases* ❧

1) When latitude equals (90° - OE) and RAMC is 270°, the horizon is completely coincident with the ecliptic. There are then no intersections of the two great circles by which to define an Ascendant. Since at all other latitudes an RAMC of 270° has an Ascendant of 0°, it would probably be safe to try it in this case. A chart with no Ascendant—is this the Invisible Man?

2) When the RAMC equals a PCED, the nearest intersection of horizon and

ecliptic to the *east* of the meridian is 180° away from it. this leaves an Asc conjunct IC and no houses I - III or VII - IX. There is room here for very creative interpretation of the data. An alternative is to consider the Asc conjunct MC, since at a PCED the MC marks a horizon/ecliptic intersection. Then the chart lacks houses X - XII and IV - VI.*

Similarly, at the North Pole (geocentric, not magnetic), the only Asc's obtainable are 0° ♈ and 0° ♎, since the horizon is also the equator, and there are only those two points of intersection with the ecliptic.

3) Also, from the North Pole, all points are south, so that Meridians, East Points, and MC's become meaningless concepts.

4) As the RAMC progresses from PCED1 to PCED2, the Ascendant longitude *recedes*. Also, for a given latitude greater than (90° - OE), no Asc will be found within the twilight zone of that latitude or among the signs opposite to it. Perhaps relocation charts of Soviet exiles to the Siberian Gulag would reveal receding Ascendants! How might this affect one's hairline? Is the native perhaps not very straight forward in his approach to situations?

*The first alternative is probably the better choice, since it at least puts the Ascendant on a degree of the ecliptic which is actually rising above the horizon. An Asc on the PCED is not rising.

Southern Hemisphere Ascendants

The same principles are used in deriving the equations for south latitude Asc calculations as were used for the north latitudes. The main difference in the calculations arises from two points: 1) In the southern hemisphere, the view is to the north, with east at the right; the apparent motions of the equator and ecliptic are counter-clockwise. 2) 90° (0° ♋) marks the low point of the declination of the ecliptic, and 270° (0° ♑) marks the high point (winter and summer solstices, respectively).

While the final equations differ slightly from those established for the northern hemisphere, a similar sequential pattern can be traced through the four quadrants.

Summary of Southern Hemisphere Asc Calculations

I. $0° \leq \text{RAEP} < 90°$ (Figure 12)

  A. $A = \arccos[-\cos(OE) \times \sin(lat) + \sin(OE) \times \cos(lat) \times \cos(RAEP)]$

  B. $\text{Asc} = \arcsin\left[\dfrac{\cos(lat) \times \sin(RAEP)}{\sin A}\right]$

II. $90° \leq \text{RAEP} < 180°$ (Figure 13)

  A. $A = \arccos[\cos(OE) \times \sin(lat) - \sin(OE) \times \cos(lat) \times \cos(RAEP)]$

  B. $\text{CRAEP} = \arccos[-\tan(OE) \times \tan(lat)]$

  C. 1) RAEP < CRAEP

   $\text{Asc} = 90° - \arccos\left[\dfrac{\cos(lat) \times \cos(RAEP - 90°)}{\sin A}\right]$

  2) RAEP = CRAEP

   $\text{Asc} = 90°$

  3) RAEP > CRAEP

   $\text{Asc} = 90° + \arccos\left[\dfrac{\cos(lat) \times \cos(RAEP - 90°)}{\sin A}\right]$

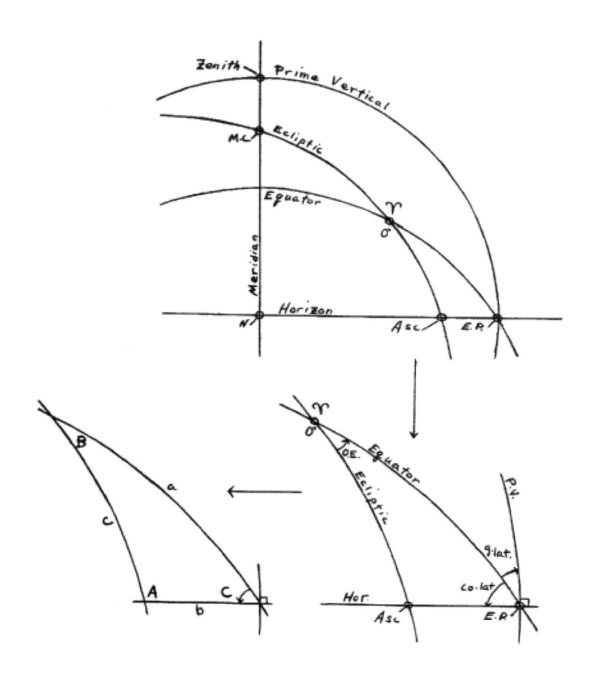

Figure 12

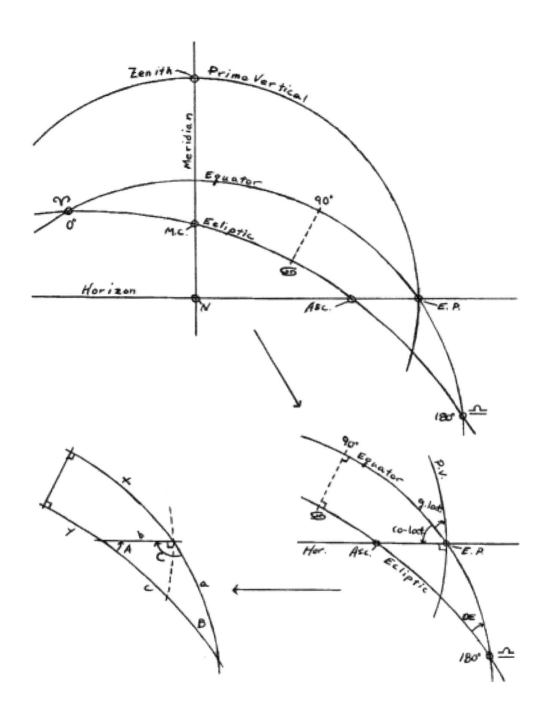

Figure 13

III. 180° ≤ RAEP < 270° (Figure 14)

    A   A = arccos [cos (OE) × sin (lat) -

             sin (OE) × cos (lat) × cos (RAEP)]

    B.   CRAEP = 360° - arccos [- tan (OE) × tan (lat)]

    C.   1)   RAEP < CRAEP

$$\text{Asc} = 180° + \arcsin \left[\frac{\cos (\text{lat}) \times \sin (\text{RAEP} - 180°)}{\sin A} \right]$$

           2)   RAEP = CRAEP

                Asc = 270°

           3)   RAEP > CRAEP

$$\text{Asc} = 360° - \arcsin \left[\frac{\cos (\text{lat}) \times \sin (\text{RAEP} - 180°)}{\sin A} \right]$$

IV. 270° ≤ RAEP < 360°/0° (Figure 15)

    A.   A = arccos [- cos (OE) × sin (lat) +

             sin (OE) × cos (lat) × cos (RAEP)]

    B. $\text{Asc} = 270° + \arccos \left[\dfrac{\cos (\text{lat}) \times \cos (\text{RAEP} - 270°)}{\sin A} \right]$

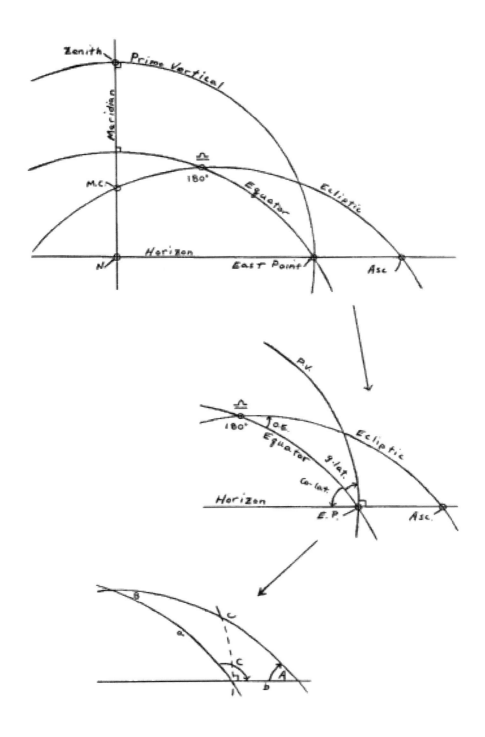

Figure 14

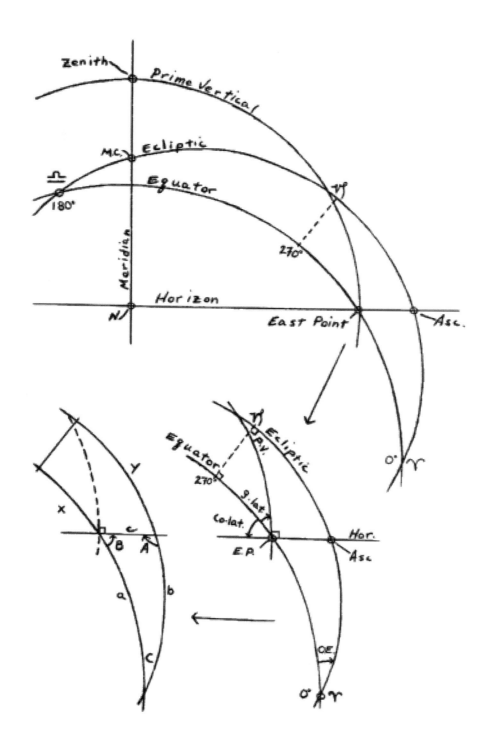

Figure 15

Antarctic Ascendant Calculations

While even fewer people are born this far south than are born above the Arctic Circle, you may want to do a solar return chart to see if a visit to the Palace of the Emperor Penguin would be of benefit. A reliable Asc and MC will be important.

These equations have been derived just as those for the north polar regions. The main difference lies in the placement of the "twilight zone" between 0° and 180° of RA. The appropriate drawings are indicated for elucidation.

Asc Calculations for South Latitude ≥ (90° - OE)

I. Find RAEP = RAMC + 90°

II. Find PCED's

    A. $Decl_h = 90° - lat$

    B. PCED calculation

        1) $PCED1 = \arcsin\left[\dfrac{\tan(decl_h)}{\tan(OE)}\right]$

        2) $PCED2 = 180° - \arcsin\left[\dfrac{\tan(decl_h)}{\tan(OE)}\right]$

III. Asc with PCED1 ≤ RAMC ≤ PCED2 (twilight zone)

    A. $A = \arccos[\cos(OE) \times \sin(lat) - \sin(OE) \times \cos \times (lat) \times \cos(RAEP)]$

    B. Asc longitude

        1) PCED1 ≤ RAMC < 90° (Figure 16)

$$Asc = 180° + \arcsin\left[\dfrac{\cos(lat) \times \sin(RAEP)}{\sin A}\right]$$

        2) RAMC = 90°

            Asc = 180°

        3) 90° < RAMC ≤ PCED2 (Figure 17)

$$Asc = 180° - \arcsin\left[\dfrac{\cos(lat) \times \sin(RAEP - 180°)}{\sin A}\right]$$

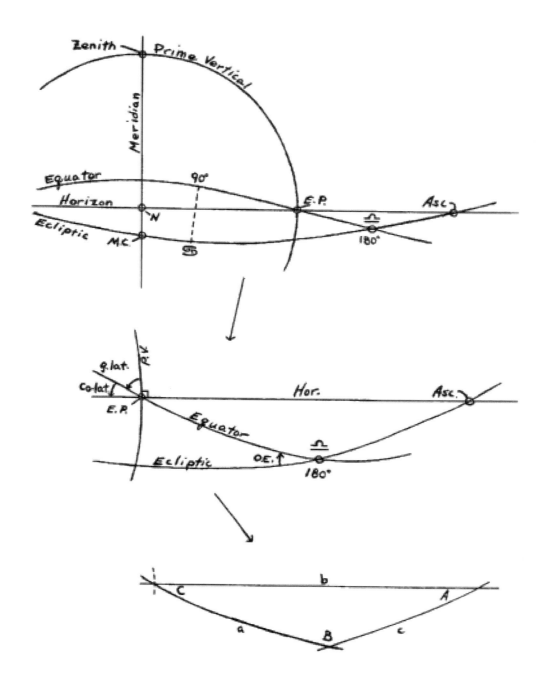

Figure 16

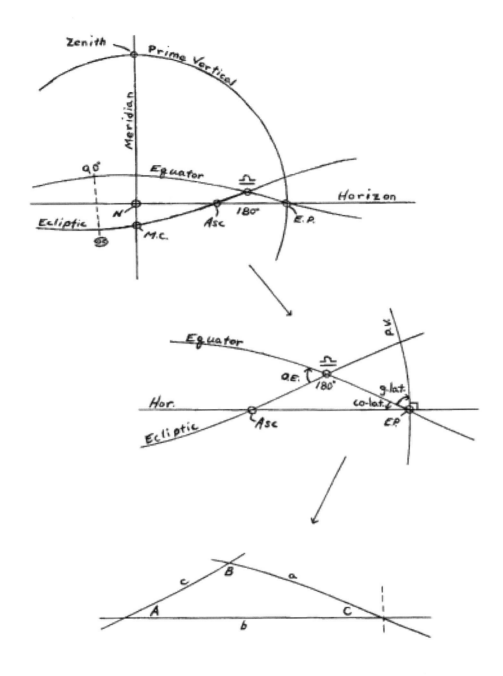

Figure 17

IV. Asc with RAMC outside twilight zone

    A. $0° \leq \text{RAEP} < 90°$, RAMC > PCED2

        1) $A = \arccos[-\cos(OE) \times \sin(lat) + \sin(OE) \times \cos(lat) \times \cos(RAEP)]$

        2) $\text{Asc} = \arcsin\left[\dfrac{\cos(lat) \times \sin(RAEP)}{\sin A}\right]$

    B. $90° \leq \text{RAEP} < 180°$

        1) $A = \arccos[\cos(OE) \times \sin(lat) - \sin(OE) \times \cos(lat) \times \cos(RAEP)]$

        2) $\text{Asc} = 90° - \arccos\left[\dfrac{\cos(lat) \times \cos(RAEP - 90°)}{\sin A}\right]$

    C. $180° \leq \text{RAEP} < 270°$

        1) $A = \arccos[\cos(OE) \times \sin(lat) - \sin(OE) \times \cos(lat) \times \cos(RAEP)]$

        2) $\text{Asc} = 360° - \arcsin\left[\dfrac{\cos(lat) \times \sin(RAEP - 180°)}{\sin A}\right]$

    D. $270° \leq \text{RAEP} < 360°/ 0°$, RAMC < PCED1

        1) $A = \arccos[-\cos(OE) \times \sin(lat) + \sin(OE) \times \cos(lat) \times \cos(RAEP)]$

        2) $\text{Asc} = 270° + \arccos\left[\dfrac{\cos(lat) \times \cos(RAEP - 270°)}{\sin A}\right]$

One encounters the same special cases in the south polar regions as in the north polar regions, and the same solutions can be attempted. In the first case noted, the problem RAMC would be 90°, with a probable Ascendant of 180°.

Examples

1) April 4, 1949; Sidereal Time $3^h 42^m 25^s$; Geographic latitude 39° **N** 45' = 39.75° **N**; OE = 23° 26' 54" = 23.448333°

   I. Geocentric lat = arctan [0.9932774 × tan (39.75°)] = 39.560115° N

   II. RAMC converted to degree measure:

   $$3^h \times 15°/h = 45° \; 00' \; 00"$$
   $$+ 42^m \times 15'/m = 10° \; 30' \; 00"$$
   $$+ 25^s \times 15"/s = \underline{\;0° \; 06' \; 15"\;}$$
   $$RAMC = 55° \; 36' \; 15" = 55.604167°$$

   III. MC longitude = $\arctan \left[\dfrac{\tan(55.604167°)}{\cos(23.448333°)} \right]$ = 57.868217°

   MC = 27° ♉ 52' 06"

   IV. Asc longitude

   A. RAEP = 55.604167° + 90° = 145.604167°

   B. A = arccos [- cos (23.448333°) × sin (39.560115°) −

   sin (23.448333°) × cos (39.560115°) × cos (145.604167°)]

   A = 109.33868°

   C. Asc = $90° + \arccos \left[\dfrac{\cos(39.560115°) \times \cos(55.604167°)}{\sin(109.33868°)} \right]$

   Asc = 152.5121° = 2° ♍ 30' 44"

2) January 14, 1935; Sidereal Time $10^h 33^m 14^s$; Geographic latitude 52° **S** 24' = 52.4° **S**;
OE = 23° 26' 56" = 23.448889°

I. Geocentric lat = 52.213013°

II. RAMC = 158° 18' 30" = 158.30833°

III. MC = 90° + arctan [cos (23.448889°) × tan (68.30833°)]

MC = 156.559047° = 6° ♍ 33' 33"

IV. Asc longitude

    A. RAEP = 158.30833° + 90° = 248.30833°

    B. A = arccos [cos (23.448889°) × sin (52.213013°) −

           sin (23.448889°) × cos (52.213013°) × cos (248.30833°)]

        A = 35.398004°

    C. CRAEP = 360° − arccos[− tan(23.448889°) × tan (52.213013°)]

        CRAEP = 235.98208°

        RAEP > CRAEP

    D. $\text{Asc} = 360° - \arcsin \left[\dfrac{\cos(52.213013°) \times \sin(68.30833°)}{\sin(35.398004°)} \right]$

        Asc = 280.61609° = 10° ♑ 36' 58"

3) July 12, 1978; Sidereal Time $12^h 22^m 38^s$; Geographic latitude 21° **N** 33' = 21.55° **N**;
OE = 23° 26' 22" = 23.439444°

I. Geocentric lat = 21.41829°

II. RAMC = 185° 39' 30" = 185.65833°

III. $MC = 180° + \arctan\left[\dfrac{\tan(5.65833°)}{\cos(23.439444°)}\right]$

MC = 186.16349° = 6° ♎ 09' 49"

IV. Asc longitude

    A. RAEP = 185.65833° + 90° = 275.65833°

    B. A = arccos [cos (23.439444°) × sin (21.41829°) +

        sin (23.439444°) × cos (21.41829°) × cos (275.65833°)]

        A = 68.188687°

    C. CRAEP = 360° - arccos [tan (23.439444°) × tan (21.41829°)]

        CRAEP = 279.7918°

        RAEP < CRAEP

    D. $Asc = 270° - \arccos\left[\dfrac{\cos(21.41829°) \times \cos(5.65833°)}{\sin(68.188687°)}\right]$

Asc = 266.2291° = 26° ♐ 13' 48"

4) November 23, 1918; Sidereal Time $22^h 47^m 07^s$;
Geographic latitude 40° S 17' = 40.283333° S; OE = 23° 27' 01" = 23.450278°

I. Geocentric lat = 40.092814°

II. RAMC = 341° 46' 45" = 341.779167°

III. MC = 270° + arctan [cos (23.450278°) × tan (71.779167°)]

　　　MC = 340.260849° = 10° ♓ 15' 39"

IV. Asc longitude

　　A. RAEP = 341.779167° + 90° = 431.779167° = 71.779167°

　　B. A = arccos [- cos (23.450278°) × sin (40.092814°) +

　　　　sin (23.450278°) × cos (40.092814°) × cos (71.779167°)]

　　　　A = 119.71222°

　　C. $\text{Asc} = \arcsin \left[\dfrac{\cos(40.092814°) \times \sin(71.779167°)}{\sin(119.71222°)} \right]$

　　　　Asc = 56.787031° = 26° ♉ 47' 13"

5) March 15, 1964; Sidereal Time $16^h\,13^m\,06^s$; Geographic latitude 72° **N** 51' = 72.85° **N**; OE = 23° 26' 37.5" = 23.44375°

    I.   Geocentric lat = 72.740801°

           90° - OE = 66.55625°

           Geocentric lat > Arctic Circle

    II.   RAMC = 243° 16' 30" = 243.275°

    III. $MC = 180° + \arctan\left[\dfrac{\tan(63.275°)}{\cos(23.44375°)}\right]$

           MC = 245.2063° = 5° ♐ 12' 23"

    IV.   PCED's

        A. $decl_h$ = 90° - 72.740801° = 17.259199°

        B.   PCED calculation

           1) $PCED1 = 180° + \arcsin\left[\dfrac{\tan(17.259199°)}{\tan(23.44375°)}\right]$

               PCED1 = 225.76196°

           2) $PCED2 = 360° - \arcsin\left[\dfrac{\tan(17.259199°)}{\tan(23.44375°)}\right]$

               PCED2 = 314.23804°

        (Since it is obvious that RAMC falls between PCED1 and 270°, step 2 of this operation is not necessary in this instance.)

        C.   PCED1 ≤ RAMC < 270°

    V.   Asc longitude

        A.   RAEP = 243.275° + 90° = 333.275°

        B.   A = arccos [cos (23.44375°) × sin (72.740801°) +

               sin (23.44375°) × cos (72.740801°) × cos (333.275°)]

           A = 11.01701°

        C. $Asc = \arcsin\left[\dfrac{-\cos(72.740801°) \times \sin(333.275°)}{\sin(11.01701°)}\right]$

           Asc = 44.282764° = 14° ♉ 16' 58"

Appendix to Part One

Occasionally (more often than astrologers care for) a horoscope is erected on a spurious birth time. As a result of various rectification procedures, an Ascendant may be derived which proves correct in regard to available dated experiences of the native. However, it may be desirable to ascertain the corresponding birth time in order to "fill out" the chart properly, and to do further work with progressions, directions and transits.

The derivation of the birth time from a hypothetical Ascendant, birth date and birth place is not difficult, but a number of steps is involved. First, spherical trigonometry is used in computation of the RAEP (Right Ascension of the East Point) from the Ascendant longitude and geocentric latitude of birth. RAEP is then used to derive Local Sidereal Time (LST). The remaining calculations are a brief excersise in equating degrees of longitude with units of time (using time to measure one's position, and visa versa); and in converting elapsed sidereal hours to elapsed mean solar (civil) hours. Sidereal time units and mean time units are treated equally when used only for measurement of position. In working with the passage of time, however, sidereal and mean time units must be reconciled with each other at the rate of 0.9972691 mean hr/ sid hr.

Data required for this operation include a rectified Ascendant, birth date, birth place (longitude and geocentric latitude), and the obliquity of the ecliptic for the period. Working in decimal fractions of degrees and hours, rather than in minutes and seconds, facilitates the process considerably. End results are then converted back to the more conventional hours/ minutes/ seconds notation. An outline of the procedure follows.

I. RAEP (or Oblique Ascension of the Ascendant degree)

    A. Asc declination = arcsin [sin (long) × sin (OE)] (Retain the algebraic sign, "+" or "-", which obtains.)

    B. Ascensional difference of the Ascendant degree (a.d.) (See *Definitions,* page 6, and Figure 3 of *Koch*, page 138, in **Part Two**.)

        a.d. = arcsin [tan (Asc decl) × tan (lat)] (Retain the algebraic sign, as above.)

    C. Right Ascension of the Ascendant degree

        1) $0° \leq \text{long} < 90°$

$$\text{RAAsc} = \arctan [\tan(\text{long}) \times \cos(\text{OE})]$$

        2) $90° \leq \text{long} < 180°$

$$\text{RAAsc} = 90° + \arctan \left[\frac{\tan(\text{long} - 90°)}{\cos(\text{OE})} \right]$$

        3) $180° \leq \text{long} < 270°$

$$\text{RAAsc} = 180° + \arctan [\tan(\text{long} - 180°) \times \cos(\text{OE})]$$

4) $270° \leq \text{long} < 360°/0°$

$$\text{RAAsc} = 270° + \arctan\left[\frac{\tan(\text{long} - 270°)}{\cos(\text{OE})}\right]$$

D. RAEP

1) North latitude: RAEP = RAAsc - a.d.
2) South latitude: RAEP = RAAsc + a.d.

II. Local Sidereal Time (LST)

A. RAMC = RAEP - 90°

B. $\text{LST} = \dfrac{\text{RAMC}}{15°/\text{hr}}$

III. MC longitude

A. $0° \leq \text{RAMC} < 90°$

$$\text{MC} = \arctan\left[\frac{\tan(\text{RAMC})}{\cos(\text{OE})}\right]$$

B. $90° \leq \text{RAMC} < 180°$

$$\text{MC} = 90° + \arctan[\tan(\text{RAMC} - 90°) \times \cos(\text{OE})]$$

C. $180° \leq \text{RAMC} < 270°$

$$\text{MC} = 180° + \arctan\left[\frac{\tan(\text{RAMC} - 180°)}{\cos(\text{OE})}\right]$$

D. $270° \leq \text{RAMC} < 360°/0°$

$$\text{MC} = 270° + \arctan[\tan(\text{RAMC} - 270°) \times \cos(\text{OE})]$$

IV. Conversion of LST to Standard Mean Time (SMT)

Note: For an explanation of the abbreviations used in the following calculations, see page 7, *Calculation of Local Sidereal Time*.

$$\text{SMT} = [(\text{LST} - \text{GSTeph} + \text{LLD}) \times (0.9972691 \text{ mean hr/ sid hr})] - \text{SLD}$$

⇨ If LST < GST, use LST + 24hours

⇨ If bracketed data < SLD, add 24hours to former

In this equation, the bracketed portion converts sidereal hours elapsed at Greenwich to standard mean hours elapsed at Greenwich. Subtracting the SLD "relocates" the converted units to the time zone of birth. SMT obtained in this calculation is actually a measure of mean hours between the time of the ephemeris entry and the birth time. The actual hour of birth is reckoned thus:

Midnight (0^h) ephemeris: Adding the SMT to the entry time of 0^h will yield the birth time in 24^h clock notation; *i.e.*, SMT is the Standard Mean Time of birth.

Noon (12^h) ephemeris: Adding the SMT to the entry time of 12^h may bring the resulting time ahead into the day following the day of the ephemeris entry used. Therefore an SMT exceeding 12^h should be reduced by that amount, the birth time then being in the AM of the following date. *Example*: SMT = 22^h; GSTeph is from noon of July 4; birth time is 10 AM on July 5. SMT of less than 12^h added to 12^h of the ephemeris will yield a birth time in 24^h clock notation.

All that remains is the adjustment of the Standard Mean Time of birth to local time conventions such as such as daylight or double daylight time. This is a simple matter of adding one or two hours, respectively, to the standard time of birth.

❧ Examples ❧

1) March 5, 1951; longitude = 74.283333°W; geocentric latitude = 40.325891° **N**; OE = 23.448333°; Asc = 24° ♋ 02', or 84.033333°

    I. RAEP

        A. Asc decl = 23.313769° (N)
        B. a.d. = 21.457417°
        C. RAAsc = 83.500657°
        D. RAEP = 62.04324°

    II. LST

        A. RAMC = 332.04324°
        B. LST = 22.136216^h

    III. MC = 329.94993°

    IV. LST to SMT

GSTeph (0^h, March 5) = 10.795556^h; LLD = 4.9522222^h; SLD = 5^h

$$SMT = [(22.136216^h - 10.795556^h + 4.9522222^h) \times (0.9972691 \text{ mean hr/ sid hr})] - 5^h$$

SMT = 11.248388^h; Birth time is 11^{h}14^{m}54^s AM, EST

Same data with noon ephemeris: GSTeph (12^h, March 4) = 22.762778^h
Increase LST by 12^h before proceeding.

$$SMT = [(46.136216^h - 22.762778^h + 4.9522222^h) \times (0.9972691 \text{ mean hr/ sid hr})] - 5^h$$

SMT = 23.248305^h elapsed from noon on March 4. Birth time is 11^{h}14^{m}54^s AM, EST.

2) May 20, 1979; longitude = 76.141667°W; geocentric latitude = 39.701511° **N**; OE = 23.439444°; Asc = 7° ♎ 23' 33", or 187.39257°

    I.   RAEP
        A.   Asc decl = − 2.9337432° (S)
        B.   a.d. = − 2.4386384°
        C.   RAAsc = 186.78849°
        D.   RAEP = 189.22713°

    II.   LST
        A.   RAMC = 99.227126°
        B.   LST = 6.615142^h

    III.   MC = 98.447261°

    IV.   LST to SMT
GSTeph (0^h, May 20) = 15.803611^h; LLD = 5.0761111^h; SLD = 5^h; Add 24^h to LST

$$SMT = [(30.615142^h - 15.803611^h + 5.0761111^h) \times (0.9972691 \text{ mean hr/ sid hr})] - 5^h$$

SMT = 14.833331^h; Birth time is $14^h 50^m$, or $2^h 50^m$ PM, EST; or, $3^h 50^m$ PM, E*D*T

Same data with noon ephemeris: GSTeph (12^h, May 20) = 3.8366667^h

$$SMT = [(6.615142^h - 3.8366667^h + 5.0761111^h) \times (0.9972691 \text{ mean hr/ sid hr})] - 5^h$$

SMT = 2.8331363^h elapsed from noon on May 20. Birth time is $2^h 49^m 59^s$ PM, EST; or, $3^h 49^m 59^s$ PM, E*D*T.

Ephemeris data in these examples are from the sources listed in *Calculation of Local Sidereal Time*, on page 9.

PART TWO

FURTHER DIVISIONS:

THE TWELVE HOUSES

Introduction

House systems: for centuries – millennia – astrologers have been, by various means, dividing the celestial sphere into units which represent fields of human development and experience. Currently there are over a dozen such systems in use. Each method for deriving house cusps from the birth or event data reflect an underlying attitude, whether conscious or not, of the practitioner toward astrology. One may compare cusps from several systems, for the same native, and, finding little discrepancy, ask "What's the difference?" The difference lies in knowing how a system operates, and whether or not the parameters used combine in a way that is meaningful to the astrologer. With this understanding of a complete horoscope, one can develop more confidence in and derive more satisfaction from the practice of astrology. One may find it helpful to use different systems for different types of interpretation, such as predictive work, or general counselling. But first it is necessary to study house systems and how they work.

The systems "dissected" here have in common several features: in each the Ascendant equals the cusp of House I, and the Midheaven is the cusp of X. These systems are also all *birthplace specific*; *i.e.*, for a given birth (or event) time, no two charts will be the same unless they are from the exact same location. This ensures a unique chart for each individual. Also, with few exceptions, the house systems chosen for treatment are operable anywhere on the globe. Not all methods of house division incorporate these characteristics.

There are, mechanically speaking, several points of differentiation among the systems included. Some are completely static (Porphyry, Campanus and Regiomontanus), while others base division of the celestial sphere on a moving point (Alcabitius and Koch). There are differences in which great circles are divided, and which moving points are measured.

I have attempted to outline philosphical points connected with these different methods of house division, but they are my own view, and the reader may have his or her own valid interpretations.

The examples given for each house system are the same as those used at the end of **Part One** for latitude, MC and Asc calculations. Those calculations are not repeated in **Part Two**.

Note -- While this manual is designed to accommodate data for either northern or southern hemisphere, the diagrams in **Part Two** represent portions of the celestial sphere viewed from the former only, facing south for the "upper" houses and north for the "lower" houses. In adapting these drawings to a southern hemisphere view, a lateral mirror imaging is required: MC to the north, IC to the south; east on the right in the former case, to the left in the latter. Also, right ascension and longitude increase clockwise viewed from south of the equator. In the diagrams, ♋ and ♑ trade places, as do ♈ and ♎. Reference to figures in **Part One** may be helpful in visualizing this.

PORPHYRY

AND

ALCABITIUS

Introduction

Why Porphyry and Alcabitius, two relatively obscure house systems? For the sake of chronology, they belong together, both being quite early. Porphyry lived in the third century AD, and Alcabitius pre-dates the first century AD. They make a good starting point for a study of house systems in western astrology.

Both of these systems offer birthplace specificity, as aforementioned; they are possibly among the earliest that do. (The calculations that follow do not directly include latitude; however, the Asc longitude, which figures into cusp calculations for these two methods, is based on geocentric latitude.)

Another characteristic shared by the Porphyry and Alcabitius methods is simplicity. Not that simplicity in itself makes for a good house system -- but it does make for a good beginning in analyzing house systems. Coupled with simplicity is universality: at only a certain few sidereal moments at latitudes greater than the Arctic and Antarctic Circles do these systems fail. For example, finding a MC and Asc at the exact North Pole is difficult when every direction is south. (These problems are discussed in *Arctic Region Asc Calculation*, on pages 38 and 39.)

A final reason for reviewing these two ancient methods of house division is that they appear to reflect two very different outlooks on the relationship of macrocosm to microcosm, or of god/s to humankind.

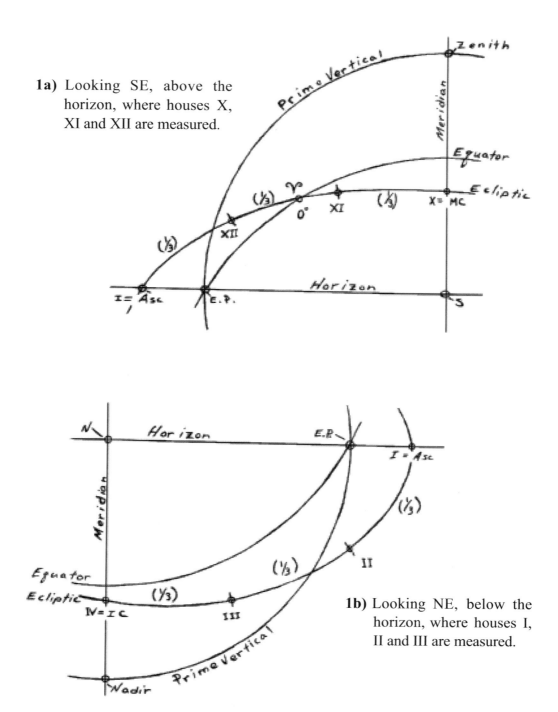

1a) Looking SE, above the horizon, where houses X, XI and XII are measured.

1b) Looking NE, below the horizon, where houses I, II and III are measured.

Figure 1: Porphyry

Porphyry

Porphyry's method for deriving house cusps is probably the simplest birthplace specific system to calculate. MC and Asc are cusps X and I, respectively. Intermediate cusps are found by trisection of the segment of the ecliptic arc between Asc and MC, giving XI and XII. Cusps II and III are obtained by similar division of the ecliptic arc from the Asc to the IC. Remaining cusps are found by adding 180° to their opposites.

Interpretations may vary, but this is my analysis of the Porphyry outlook: The ecliptic, marking the orbital plane of the earth, is roughly aligned with the plane of the solar system. From a geocentric point of view it is along the ecliptic that most celestial events take place. It is, in a manner of speaking, the realm or source of divine influences. The primary physical being of the native, as represented by the Ascendant, results from the interaction of the celestial and the mundane (ecliptic and horizon). The native's life experiences, however, as delineated by the house cusps, are completely under celestial influence--there is no worldly intermediary element (equator, prime vertical, horizon) involved in their derivations. The mystical number 3 also remains unaffected by mundane influence--the three houses in each quadrant are equal in size. Thus Porphyry seems to present through his method a rather fatalistic outlook.

❧ Calculations ☙

I. Cusps XI and XII (Figure 1a, facing page)
   A. Determine ecliptic arc from Asc to MC
      arc = Asc - MC
      or, for MC > Asc
      arc = (Asc + 360°) - MC
   B. Trisect arc
   C. Obtain cusps
      1) XI = MC + $^1/_3$ arc
      2) XII = XI + $^1/_3$ arc
      (Any value over 360° is to be reduced by 360°)

II. Cusps II and III (Figure 1b)
   A. Determine ecliptic arc from Asc to IC
      arc = IC - Asc *or* arc = (IC + 360°) - Asc
      ⇨ Since MC and IC are 180° apart, this lower ecliptic arc can also be obtained by
      lower arc = 180° - upper arc

        B.   Trisect arc

        C.   Obtain cusps

            1)   II = Asc + $\frac{1}{3}$ arc

            2)   III = II + $\frac{1}{3}$ arc

III.   Remaining cusps: Add 180° to each known cusp to obtain its opposite.

Note--Equations for calculating Porphyry houses for the southern hemisphere are the same as above. Of course, Asc must first be correctly calculated for south latitude.

❧ Examples ❦

1) April 4, 1949; ST = $3^h 42^m 25^s$; OE = 23.448333°;
   geocentric latitude = 39.560115° N; MC = 57.868217°; Asc = 152.5121°

   I. Cusps XI and XII

       A. Ecliptic arc from Asc to MC

          upper arc = 152.5121° - 57.868217° = 94.643883°

       B. Trisected arc = 31.547961°

       C. Cusps

          XI = 57.868217° + 31.547961° = 89.416178°

          XII = 89.416178° + 31.547961° = 120.964139°

   II. Cusps II and III

       A. Ecliptic arc from Asc to IC

          lower arc = 180° - upper arc = 85.356117°

       B. Trisected arc = 28.452039°

       C. Cusps

          II = 152.5121° + 28.452039° = 180.9641°

          III = 180.9641° + 28.452039° = 209.4161°

   III Summary

X/MC	= 27° ♉ 52' 06"	IV/IC	= 27° ♏ 52' 06"
XI	= 29° ♊ 24' 58"	V	= 29° ♐ 24' 58"
XII	= 0° ♌ 57' 51"	VI	= 0° ♒ 57' 51"
I/Asc	= 2° ♍ 30' 44"	VII/Desc	= 2° ♓ 30' 44"
II	= 0° ♎ 57' 51"	VIII	= 0° ♈ 57' 51"
III	= 29° ♎ 24' 58"	IX	= 29° ♈ 24' 58"

   ♋ and ♑ intercepted

2)   January 14, 1935; ST = $10^h 33^m 14^s$; OE = 23.448889°;

geocentric latitude = 52.213013° S; MC = 156.559047; Asc = 280.61609°

   I.   Cusps XI and XII

      A.   Ecliptic arc from Asc to MC

          upper arc = 280.61609° − 156.559047° = 124.05704°

      B.   Trisected arc = 41.352347°

      C.   Cusps

          XI = 156.559047° + 41.352347° = 197.9114°

          XII = 197.9114° + 41.352347° = 239.26374°

  II.   Cusps II and III

      A.   Ecliptic arc from ASC to IC

          lower arc = 180° − 124.05704° = 55.94296°

      B.   Trisected arc = 18.647653°

      C.   Cusps

          II = 280.61609° + 18.647653° = 299.26374°

          III = 299.26374° + 18.647653° = 317.9114°

 III.   Summary

X/MC	= 6° ♍ 33' 33"		IV/IC	= 6° ♓ 33' 33"
XI	= 17° ♎ 54' 10"		V	= 17° ♈ 54' 10"
XII	= 29° ♏ 15' 49"		VI	= 29° ♉ 15' 49"
I/Asc	= 10° ♑ 36' 58"		VII/Desc	= 10° ♋ 36' 58"
II	= 29° ♑ 15' 49"		VIII	= 29° ♋ 15' 49"
III	= 17° ♒ 54' 10"		IX	= 17° ♌ 54' 10"

♊ and ♐ intercepted

3) July 12, 1978; ST = $12^h 22^m 38^s$; OE = 23.439444°;
geocentric latitude = 21.41829° **N**; MC = 186.16349°; Asc = 266.22991°

    I.   Cusps XI and XII

        A.   Upper arc = 80.06561°

        B.   Trisected arc = 26.688537°

        C.   Cusps

            XI = 212.85203°

            XII = 239.54056°

    II.   Cusps II and III

        A.   Lower arc = 99.93439°

        B.   Trisected arc = 33.311463°

        C.   Cusps

            II = 299.54056°

            III = 332.85203°

    III.   Summary

X/MC	= 6° ♎ 09' 49"	IV/IC	= 6° ♈ 09' 49"
XI	= 2° ♏ 51' 07"	V	= 2° ♉ 51' 07"
XII	= 29° ♏ 32' 26"	VI	= 29° ♉ 32' 26"
I/Asc	= 26° ♐ 13' 45"	VII	= 26° ♊ 13' 45"
II	= 29° ♑ 32' 26"	VIII	= 29° ♋ 32' 26"
III	= 2° ♓ 51' 07"	IX	= 2° ♍ 51' 07"

♌ and ♒ intercepted

4) November 23, 1918; ST = $22^h 47^m 07^s$; OE = 23.450278°;
geocentric latitude = 40.092814° **S**; MC = 340.260849°; Asc = 56.78703°

    I.   Cusps XI and XII

        A.   Upper arc = 416.78703° - 340.26085° = 76.526181°

        B.   Trisected arc = 25.508727°

        C.   Cusps

            XI = 365.76958° = 5.76958°

            XII = 31.278304°

    II.   Cusps II and III

        A.   Lower arc = 103.47382°

        B.   Trisected arc = 34.491273°

        C.   Cusps

            II = 91.278304°

            III = 125.76958°

    III.   Summary

X/MC	= 10° ♓ 15' 39"	IV/IC	=	10° ♍ 15' 39"
XI	= 5° ♈ 46' 10"	V	=	5° ♎ 46' 10"
XII	= 1° ♉ 16' 42"	VI	=	1° ♏ 16' 42"
I/Asc	= 26° ♉ 47' 13"	VII/Desc	=	26° ♏ 47' 13"
II	= 1° ♋ 16' 42"	VIII	=	1° ♑ 16' 42"
III	= 5° ♌ 46' 10"	IX	=	5° ♒ 46' 10"

        ♊ and ♐ intercepted

5) March 15, 1964; ST = $16^h\ 13^m\ 06^s$; OE = 23.44375°;
geocentric latitude = 72.740801° **N**; MC = 245.2063°; Asc = 44.282764°

    I.   Cusps XI and XII

        A.   Upper arc = 159.07646°

        B.   Trisected arc = 53.025488°

        C.   Cusps

            XI = 298.23179°

            XII = 351.25728°

    II.   Cusps II and III

        A.   Lower arc = 20.92354°

        B.   Trisected arc = 6.974513°

        C.   Cusps

            II = 51.257277°

            III = 58.231791°

    III.   Summary

X/MC	= 5° ♐ 12' 23"	IV/IC	= 5° ♊ 12' 23"
XI	= 28° ♑ 13' 54"	V	= 28° ♋ 13' 54"
XII	= 21° ♓ 15' 26"	VI	= 21° ♍ 15' 26"
I/Asc	= 14° ♉ 16' 58"	VII/Desc	= 14° ♏ 16' 58"
II	= 21° ♉ 15' 26"	VIII	= 21° ♏ 15' 26"
III	= 28° ♉ 13' 54"	IX	= 28° ♏ 13' 54"

♈, ♌, ♎, ♒ intercepted

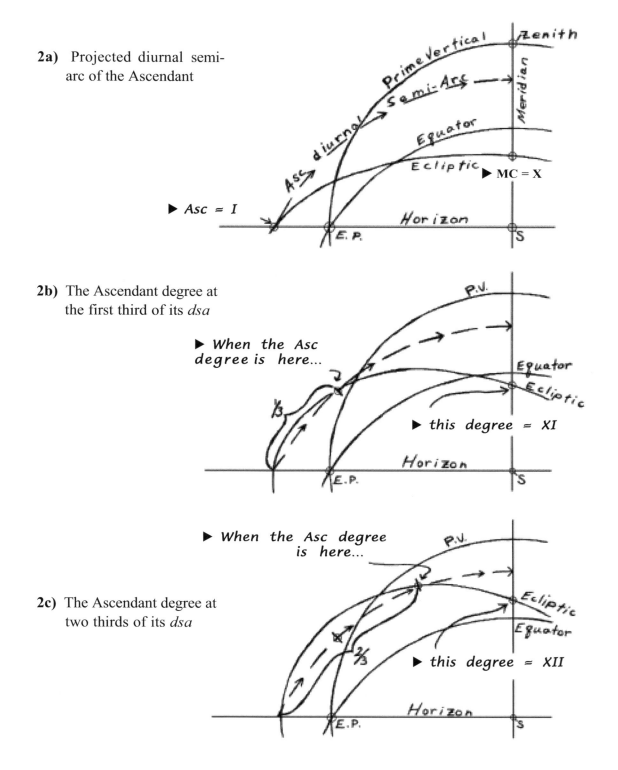

Figure 2: Alcabitius

Alcabitius

Every body in the heavens has a daily apparent circular path about the earth caused by the earth's rotation. This circadian route is divided into the *diurnal* arc, "visible" above the horizon; and the *nocturnal* arc, which lies below the horizon. These arcs are further divided into *semi-arcs* from horizon to meridian. A body's diurnal semi-arc plus its nocturnal semi-arc (both from the same side of the meridian) add up to 180°.

Every degree of the ecliptic likewise has its own circadian path. Alcabitius' method of house division uses segments of the diurnal arc of the Ascendant degree of the ecliptic to establish house cusps. The diurnal semi-arc (from east horizon to meridian) is trisected; the divisions mark stations, the Ascendant's advancement to which marks the transits of cusps XI and XII at the meridian. Similar divisions of the western diurnal semi-arc mark stations the Ascendant degree attains when cusps VIII and IX transit the lower branch of the meridian (where the IC is located at the birth time). "Time" is marked at the fixed meridian in terms of house cusps.

The divisions of the ecliptic by Alcabitius being made through the intermediary of the processing Ascendant, this system suggests to me that the native, as represented by the Ascendant, has some degree of input into the effects of divine/cosmic influence on his development and life experiences. There is, necessarily, a cosmic plan, represented by the celestial motions giving rise to the house divisions, to which one must adhere. Nevertheless -- and seemingly paradoxically -- the native may have a consciousness of a role in shaping his experiences. This concept has been part of the great debates on free will and its operation.

Calculations

Derivation of Alcabitius' cusps is more involved than the Porphyry method. A problem that arises is that the circadian circle is not a great circle, but a parallel of declination, analogous to parallels of latitude. It is not subject to the regular laws of spherical trigonometry. A more thorough description of the Alcabitius method, first related to me by Al H. Morrison, may aid in analyzing the task at hand.

Imagine the Ascendant on its diurnal trek in motion from horizon to meridian after the birth time (Figure 2a, facing page). When the Ascendant has covered one-third of its semi-arc, the ecliptic degree on the meridian is that of cusp XI (Figure 2b). When the Ascendant has traversed two-thirds of its eastern semi-arc, the ecliptic degree on the meridian is that of cusp XII (Figure 2c).

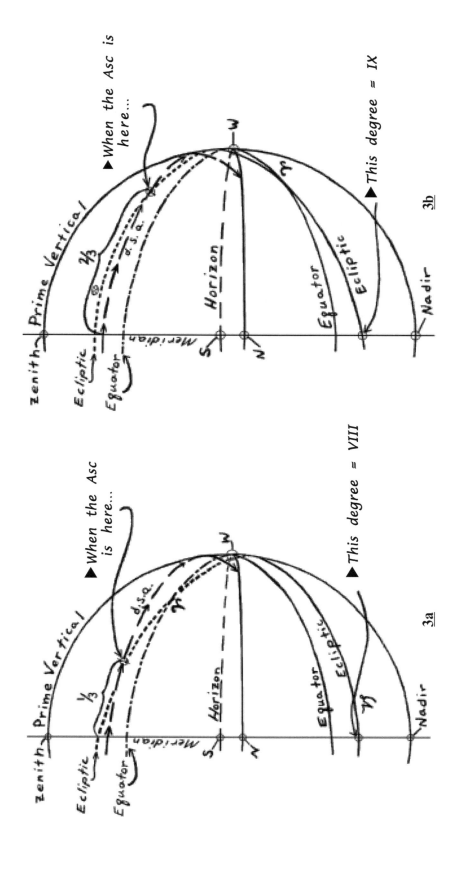

Figure 3: Alcabitius

These drawings represent half the celestial sphere viewed through the Prime Vertical, looking straight at the Meridian. The equator, ecliptic and horizon are seen against the far side of the sphere as broken lines; they curve around the west point of the Prime Vertical and onto the near side of the celestial sphere. Figure 3a locates the Ascendant on its diurnal arc and cusp VIII transiting the meridian; Figure 3b locates the Ascendant and cusp IX.

When the Ascendant reaches the one-third point on its path from culmination to setting, the degree of the ecliptic on the lower branch of the meridian is the cusp of house VIII (Figure 3a). The cusp of IX crosses the lower meridian as the Ascendant attains the second third of its semi-arc toward the western horizon (Figure 3b). Remaining cusps are found by adding 180° to their opposites; cusps I and X are the Ascendant and Midheaven, respectively.

A closer look at the workings of this system can eliminate the problem of the parallel circles and lead to a simpler mathematical description of house cusp locations. Note that the house cusps are marked at the meridian. Since the meridian is coincident with celestial hour circles, the Alcabitius house circles will also be coincident with hour circles. Thus, a house cusp's transit of the meridian marks not only its longitude, but also its right ascension along the celestial equator, which is, helpfully, a great circle. The next step is to define the diurnal semi-arc in terms of degrees of right ascension.

Reading into the description above, it is apparent that when the Ascendant transits the meridian, it marks its own longitude, and also its own right ascension (which is not the same as the East Point!). Since the MC and RAMC lie on the meridian at the outset of the Ascendant's diurnal procession, the diurnal semi-arc can now be expressed in terms of RAAsc and RAMC, the two end points of the Ascendant arc translated from a parallel of declination to the equator. Trisecting this right ascensional arc, one obtains points of the celestial equator which will cross the meridian at the specified times in the procession of the Ascendant across the southeastern sky. This simplifies matters by reducing a moving point exercise to finding the birth time locations of the Ascendant's projected stations.

The southwestern houses of the chart, VIII and IX, have been defined in terms of the lower branch of the meridian. This is so because the system has been described in terms of a point of the ecliptic which has traversed the southern sky, the whole ecliptic, of course, going with it, so that the potential southwestern house cusps are well into the next quadrant (northwest) of the celestial sphere before they are to be marked at the meridian. As with cusps XI and XII, it is possible to find the right ascension of VIII and IX without going through the motions, so to speak. Note that when the Ascendant is on the upper branch of the meridian, the Descendant must be on the lower branch; its longitude and right ascension are marked there. When the Ascendant sets, logically cusp X, the MC, is at the lower branch of the meridian, where its right ascension is also marked. Therefore, the equatorial arc on which are marked the right ascension of cusps VIII and IX lies between the RAMC and RADesc.

Thus far we have two diurnal semi-arcs defined in terms of degrees of right ascension:

arc for XI and XII = RAAsc - RAMC

arc for VIII and IX = RAMC − RADesc

The number of parameters needed to generate Alcabitius house cusps can be reduced as follows:

$$\text{RADesc} = \text{RAAsc} - 180°$$

$$\text{arc (VIII, IX)} = \text{RAMC} - \text{RADesc}$$

Substituting,

$$\text{arc (VIII, IX)} = \text{RAMC} - (\text{RAAsc} - 180°)$$

$$= \text{RAMC} - \text{RAAsc} + 180°$$

$$= 180° - (\text{RAAsc} - \text{RAMC})$$

$$\text{arc (VIII, IX)} = 180° - \text{arc (XI, XII)}$$

For brevity, let us call arc (XI, XII) "dsa" for "diurnal semi-arc". Arc (VIII, IX) must then be equivalent to the Ascendant's nocturnal semi-arc (nsa), the supplement of the dsa. Thus

$$\text{dsa} = \text{RAAsc} - \text{RAMC}$$

$$\text{nsa} = 180° - \text{dsa}$$

Following is a summary of the equations for Alcabitius house cusps, including conversion of ecliptic longitude to right ascension, and visa versa. Keep in mind that, while "dsa" and "nsa" stand for diurnal and nocturnal semi-arcs, what we are actually using is the right ascensional equivalents of those arcs, which have been "translated" from a parallel of declination to the celestial equator. Also, the conventional method of determining house cusps by any system is to calculate cusps II and III, rather than VIII and IX. The summary holds with this convention by adding thirds of the nsa to the RAAsc, instead of subtracting the same quantities from the RAMC.

❧ *Summary* ☙

I. Find RAAsc (Figure 4)

    A. $0° \leq \text{long} < 90°$

$$\text{RA} = \arctan[\tan(\text{long}) \times \cos(\text{OE})]$$

    B. $90° \leq \text{long} < 180°$

$$\text{RA} = 90° + \arctan\left[\frac{\tan(\text{long} - 90°)}{\cos(\text{OE})}\right]$$

    C. $180° \leq \text{long} < 270°$

$$\text{RA} = 180° + \arctan[\tan(\text{long} - 180°) \times \cos(\text{OE})]$$

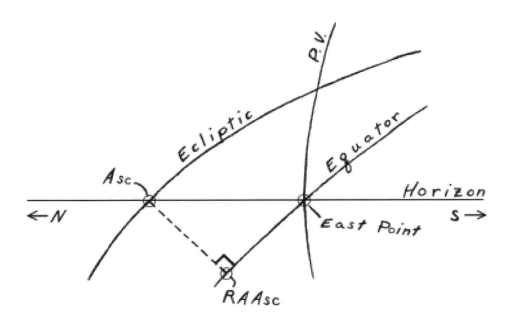

4a) RA of a summer sign Ascendant. Equatorial arc from meridian to East Point is 90°; dsa of Asc will be more than 90°.

* * * * *

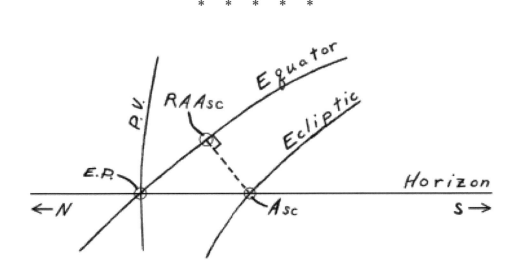

4b) RA of a winter sign Ascendant. The dsa of the Asc will be less than 90°.

Figure 4: RA Asc

D. $270° \leq \text{long} < 360°/0°$

$$RA = 270° + \arctan\left[\frac{\tan(\text{long} - 270°)}{\cos(OE)}\right]$$

II. Cusps XI and XII

   A. dsa = RAAsc - RAMC *or* dsa = (360° + RAAsc) - RAMC

   B. Trisect dsa

   C. RA of cusps

   1) RAXI = RAMC + ($^1/_3$ dsa)

   2) RAXII = RAXI + ($^1/_3$ dsa)

   D. Cusp longitude

   1) $0° \leq RA < 90°$

   $$\text{long} = \arctan\left[\frac{\tan(RA)}{\cos(OE)}\right]$$

   2) $90° \leq RA < 180°$

   long = 90° + arctan [tan (RA - 90°) × cos (OE)]

   3) $180° \leq RA < 270°$

   $$\text{long} = 180° + \arctan\left[\frac{\tan(RA - 180°)}{\cos(OE)}\right]$$

   4) $270° \leq RA < 360°/0°$

   long = 270° + arctan [tan (RA - 270°) × cos (OE)]

III. Cusps II and III

   A. nsa = 180° - dsa

   B. Trisect nsa

   C. RA of cusps

   1) RAII = RAAsc + ($^1/_3$ nsa)

   2) RAIII = RAII + ($^1/_3$ nsa)

   D. Cusp longitude: proceed as for XI and XII.

IV. Remaining cusps: Add 180° to known cusps to obtain their opposites.

Note--Equations for calculating Alcabitius houses for the southern hemisphere are the same as above. Of course, Asc must first be correctly calculated for south latitude.

❧ *Examples* ❦

1) April 4, 1949; ST = $3^h 42^m 25^s$; OE = 23.448333°; geocentric latitude = 39.560115° **N**; RAMC = 55.604167°; MC = 57.868217°; Asc = 152.5121°

   I. $\text{RAAsc} = 90° + \arctan\left[\dfrac{\tan(62.5121°)}{\cos(23.448333°)}\right] = 154.48336°$

   II. Cusps XI and XII

       A. dsa = 154.48336° - 55.604167° = 98.879193°

       B. $^1/_3$ dsa = 32.959731°

       C. RA of cusps

           1) RAXI = 55.604167° + 32.959731° = 88.563898°

           2) RAXII = 88.563898° + 32.959731° = 121.52363°

       D. Cusps

           1) $\text{XI} = \arctan\left[\dfrac{\tan(88.563898°)}{\cos(23.448333°)}\right] = 88.68245°$

           2) XII = 90° + arctan [tan (31.52363°) × cos (23.448333°)]
   XII = 119.36715°

   III. Cusps II and III

       A. nsa = 180° - 98.879195° = 81.120807°

       B. $^1/_3$ nsa = 27.040269°

       C. RA of cusps

           1) RAII = 154.48336° + 27.040269° = 181.52363°

           2) RAIII = 181.52363° + 27.040269° = 208.5639°

       D. Cusps

           1) $\text{II} = 180° + \arctan\left[\dfrac{\tan(1.52363°)}{\cos(23.448333°)}\right] = 181.6607°$

           2) $\text{III} = 180° + \arctan\left[\dfrac{\tan(28.5639°)}{\cos(23.448333°)}\right] = 210.68508°$

   IV. Summary

X/MC	= 27° ♉ 52' 06"	IV/IC	= 27° ♏ 52' 06"
XI	= 28° ♊ 40' 57"	V	= 28° ♐ 40' 57"
XII	= 29° ♋ 22' 02"	VI	= 29° ♑ 22' 02"
I/Asc	= 2° ♍ 30' 44"	VII/Desc	= 2° ♓ 30' 44"
II	= 1° ♎ 39' 39"	VIII	= 1° ♈ 39' 39"
III	= 0° ♏ 41' 06"	IX	= 0° ♉ 41' 06"

   ♌ and ♒ intercepted

2) January 14, 1935; ST = $10^h 33^m 14^s$; OE = 23.448889°;
geocentric latitude = 52.213013° S; RAMC = 158.30833°; MC = 156.559047°
Asc = 280.61609°

I. $\text{RAAsc} = 270° + \arctan\left[\dfrac{\tan(10.61609°)}{\cos(23.448889°)}\right] = 281.547088°$

II. Cusps XI and XII
   A. dsa = 281.547088° − 158.30833° = 123.23876°
   B. $^1/_3$ dsa = 41.079587°
   C. RA of cusps
      1) RAXI = 158.30833° + 41.079587° = 199.38792°
      2) RAXII = 199.38792° + 41.079587° = 240.4675°
   D. Cusps
      1) $\text{XI} = 180° + \arctan\left[\dfrac{\tan(19.38792°)}{\cos(23.448889°)}\right] = 200.98671°$
      2) $\text{XII} = 180° + \arctan\left[\dfrac{\tan(60.46751°)}{\cos(23.448889°)}\right] = 242.53749°$

III. Cusps II and III
   A. nsa = 180° − 123.23876° = 56.76124°
   B. $^1/_3$ nsa = 18.920413°
   C. RA of cusps
      1) RAII = 281.547088° + 18.920413° = 300.4675°
      2) RAIII = 300.4675° + 18.920413° = 319.38792°
   D. Cusps
      1) II = 270° + arctan [tan (30.4675°) × cos (23.448889°)]
         II = 298.35566°
      2) III = 270° + arctan [tan (49.38792°) × cos (23.448889°)]
         III = 316.9344°

IV. Summary

X/MC	=	6° ♍ 33' 33"	IV/IC	=	6° ♓ 33' 33"
XI	=	20° ♎ 59' 12"	V	=	20° ♈ 59' 12"
XII	=	2° ♐ 32' 15"	VI	=	2° ♊ 32' 15"
I/Asc	=	10° ♑ 36' 58"	VII/Desc	=	10° ♋ 36' 58"
II	=	28° ♑ 21' 20"	VIII	=	28° ♋ 21' 20"
III	=	16° ♒ 56' 04"	IX	=	16° ♌ 56' 04"

♉ and ♏ intercepted

3) July 12, 1978; ST = $12^h 22^m 38^s$; OE = 23.439444°;
geocentric latitude = 21.41829° **N**; RAMC = 185.65833° MC = 186.16349°;
Asc = 266.2291°

I. RAAsc = 180° + arctan [tan (86.2291°) × cos (23.439444°)]

   RAAsc = 265.89106°

II. Cusps XI and XII

   A. dsa = 265.89106 - 185.65833° = 80.23273°

   B. $^1/_3$ dsa = 26.744243°

   C. RA of cusps
   1) RAXI = 212.40257°
   2) RAXII = 239.14682°

   D. Cusps
   1) XI = 214.67417°
   2) XII = 241.27359°

III. Cusps II and III

   A. nsa = 99.76727°

   B. $^1/_3$ nsa = 33.255757°

   C. RA cusps
   1) RAII = 299.14682°
   2) RAIII = 332.40257°

   D. Cusps
   1) II = 297.09637°
   2) III = 330.32789°

IV. Summary

X/MC	= 6° ♎ 09' 49"	IV/IC	= 6° ♈ 09' 49"
XI	= 4° ♏ 40' 27"	V	= 4° ♉ 40' 27"
XII	= 1° ♐ 16' 25"	VI	= 1° ♊ 16' 25"
I/Asc	= 26° ♐ 13' 45"	VII/Desc	= 26° ♊ 13' 45"
II	= 27° ♑ 05' 47"	VIII	= 27° ♋ 05' 47"
III	= 0° ♒ 19' 40"	IX	= 0° ♌ 19' 40"

♍ and ♓ intercepted

4) November 23, 1918; ST = $22^h 47^m 07^s$; OE = 23.450278°;
geocentric latitude = 40.092814° **S**; RAMC = 341.779167°;
MC = 340.260849°; Asc = 56.78703°

    I.   RAAsc = 54.486516°

    II.   Cusps XI and XII
- A.   dsa = 414.486516° - 341.779167° = 72.707346°
- B. $^1/_3$ dsa = 24.235782°
- C.   RA of cusps
  1) RAXI = 366.01495° = 6.01495°
  2) RAXII = 30.250734°
- D.   Cusps
  1) XI = 6.5519606°
  2) XII = 32.444346°

    III.   Cusps II and III
- A.   nsa = 107.29265°
- B. $^1/_3$ nsa = 35.764218°
- C.   RA of cusps
  1) RAII = 90.250734°
  2) RAIII = 126.01495°
- D.   Cusps
  1) II = 90.23003°
  2) III = 123.69933°

    IV.   Summary

X/MC	= 10° ♓ 15' 39"		IV/IC	= 10° ♍ 15' 39"
XI	= 6° ♈ 33' 07"		V	= 6° ♎ 33' 07"
XII	= 2° ♉ 26' 40"		VI	= 2° ♏ 26' 40"
I/Asc	= 26° ♉ 47' 13"		VII/Desc	= 26° ♏ 47' 13"
II	= 0° ♋ 13' 48"		VIII	= 0° ♑ 13' 48"
III	= 3° ♌ 41' 58"		IX	= 3° ♒ 41' 58"

♊ and ♐ intercepted

5) March 15, 1964; ST = $16^h\,13^m\,06^s$; OE = 23.44375°;
geocentric latitude = 72.740801° N; RAMC = 243.275°; MC = 245.2063°;
Asc = 44.282764°

I. RAAsc = 41.821046°

II. Cusps XI and XII

    A. dsa = 401.821046° - 243.275° = 158.54605°

    B. $^1/_3$ dsa = 52.848682°

    C. RA of cusps

        1) RAXI = 296.12368°

        2) RAXII = 348.97236°

    D. Cusps

        1) XI = 294.22417°

        2) XII = 348.00772°

III. Cusps II and III

    A. nsa = 21.45395°

    B. $^1/_3$ nsa = 7.1513167°

    C. RA of cusps

        1) RAII = 48.972363°

        2) RAIII = 56.123679°

    D. Cusps

        1) II = 51.399446°

        2) III = 58.368952°

IV. Summary

X/MC	= 5° ♐ 12' 23"		IV/IC	= 56° ♊ 12' 23"
XI	= 24° ♑ 13' 27"		V	= 24° ♋ 13' 27"
XII	= 18° ♓ 00' 28"		VI	= 18° ♍ 00' 28"
I/Asc	= 14° ♉ 16' 58"		VII/Desc	= 14° ♏ 16' 58"
II	= 21° ♉ 23' 58"		VIII	= 21° ♏ 23' 58"
III	= 28° ♉ 22' 08"		IX	= 28° ♏ 22' 08"

♈, ♌, ♎, ♒ intercepted

CAMPANUS

AND

REGIOMONTANUS

Introduction

The Campanus and Regiomontanus house systems, developed in the middle ages, offer two birthplace specific methods of house division worth analyzing. Each is within the grasp of the astrologer-mathematician, though somewhat more complex than the previously derived systems. Whereas the more simply computed houses of Porphyry and Alcabitius utilize great circles of ecliptic longitude and right ascension, respectively, these present methods make use of great circles more closely related to the horizon in the calculations. Each house circle crosses the prime vertical at right angles, with all circles employed (including horizon and meridian) mutually intersecting at the north and south points of the horizon. These two points, then, serve as poles for the Campanus and Regiomontanus systems, where Alcabitius uses the equatorial poles and Porphyry uses the ecliptic plane. In the two systems under discussion here, the two intersections of each house circle with the ecliptic mark the cusp of a given house circle and its opposite. Angular house cusps are coincident with the MC-IC and Asc-Desc axes of the nativity.

Although these two house systems have a similar mechanical basis, cusp longitudes nevertheless differ from one to the other, more so as geocentric latitude increases. The source of the difference lies in the use of two distinct methods of determining the angular separation of intermediate house circles from the meridian. Along with the mathematical difference comes a subtle interpretational difference underlying each of these methods of house division.

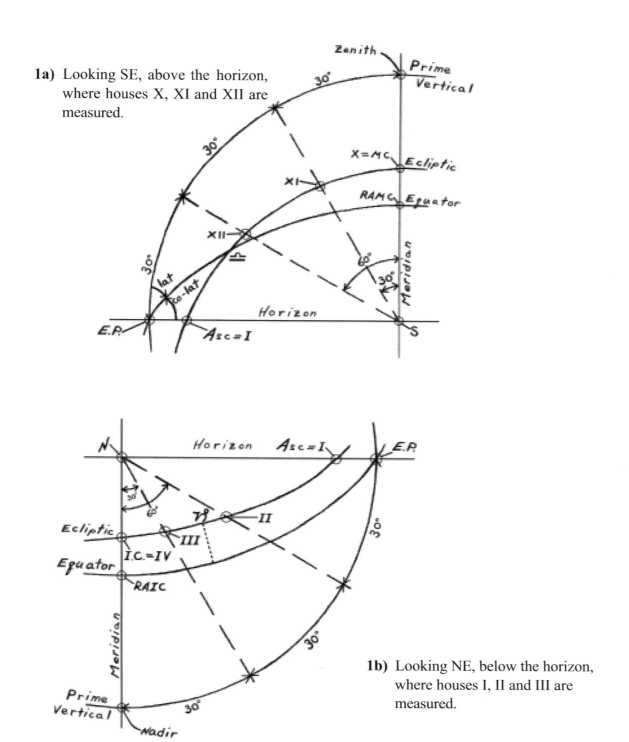

1a) Looking SE, above the horizon, where houses X, XI and XII are measured.

1b) Looking NE, below the horizon, where houses I, II and III are measured.

Figure 1: Campanus

Campanus

The Campanus house system (Figures 1a and 1b, facing page) first trisects the prime vertical from zenith to east point, and then from east point to nadir. Intermediate house circles thus divide each quadrant of the celestial sphere between meridian and horizon into three equal segments, or lunes. Each house circle intersects the ecliptic at two points 180° apart, marking two opposite house cusps.

The foundation of the Campanus method is a geodetic co-ordinate system composed of horizon, meridian and prime vertical. These three elements form an imaginary "cross-hair" against the background of the celestial sphere and centered at the zenith over any given birth or event location. While other methods of house division also utilize these co-ordinates in establishing the angular houses, Campanus computes all house cusps directly from this geodetic "target". A possible implication of this system is that apportionment of cosmic influences on the human experiences denoted by the houses is strictly the consequence of birthplace; no other elements of celestial mechanics enter into the determination of the Campanus cusp longitudes. The system has a very rational appearance.

Calculation of Campanus is not as straight forward as describing it. The house circles are not standard elements of any co-ordinate system of geodetic or celestial basis. However, a careful study of schematic drawings of Campanus divisions of the celestial sphere yields this fruit: each house circle can be treated as a "quasi-horizon", a great circle intersecting the meridian obliquely at the north and south, (rather than at right angles) 90° from the zenith. Each house cusp can therefore be calculated as a "quasi-ascendant". It is possible to determine parameters analogous to those required for computation of ascendants (refer to Figures 1 and 2):

1) **Oblique ascension of a house cusp (OAHC)**: Oblique ascension of any body or point is that degree of the celestial equator crossing the horizon simultaneously with that body. The right ascension of the east point marks the oblique ascension of the Ascendant, for example. Knowing the angular separation of a house circle from the meridian allows us to calculate the oblique ascension for each house cusp *qua* Ascendant. (Technically this measure is not true oblique ascension of the house cusps, owing to two different poles of rotation for equator and house system. A more correct term might be "quasi-oblique ascension", but for the sake of paperwork reduction I choose to abbreviate.)

2) **Quasi-latitude of a house circle (QHC)**: At the east point of the horizon the angle between the equator and the prime vertical equals the geocentric latitude. Likewise, at the intersection of a house circle with the celestial equator, the angle between the equator and a perpendicular to the house circle is analogous to latitude (compare latitude and co-latitude in Figure 1a with angles Q and B in Figure 2c). Calculation of this angle yields another parameter for computation of house cusps.

3) **Angle of the ecliptic to a house circle (A)**: As with Ascendant calculation, this angle must be found in order to solve an oblique spherical triangle one side of which measures cusp longitude. It is *not* the angle A of the right spherical triangle referred to in calculation of OAHC and QHC, but is related in function to the angle A used in Asc calculation. (See *Ascendant Longitude Calculation,* page 21 *et seq.*)

A brief analysis of the derivation of equations for the above parameters follows. Note that in abbreviations I have used the suffix "-HC" as a generic for any house circle. Specific house circles are indicated by suffixing their Roman numeral; *e.g.*, OAHC, OAXII.

❧ Calculations ❦

I. OAHC

Figures 2a and b are schematics of the southeast quadrant of the celestial sphere (above the horizon) illustrating the interrelationship of the equator, meridian and Campanus house circle. The equal 30° arcs into which this quadrant of the prime vertical (not shown) is divided are subtended by 30° angles at the south point of the horizon. The arc of the meridian from horizon to equator is subtended by the co-latitudinal angle at the east point and is equal to it. The equator crosses the meridian in a right angle. A right spherical triangle obtains (Figure 2c), with a known side and angle. Solving the triangle for a second side, an arc of the equator, gives us the OAHC as follows:

In triangle ABC, A = 30° for house circles XI and III, 60° for XII and II; B = complement of QHC; C = 90°; a = (OAHC - RAMC); b = geocentric co-latitude.

$$\tan a = \sin b \times \tan A$$

Since b = co-latitude,

$$\sin b = \sin (\text{co-lat}) = \cos (\text{lat})$$

Substituting, we get

$$\tan a = \cos (\text{lat}) \times \tan A$$

Arc a is measured in right ascension from the meridian, so that

$$a = \text{OAHC} - \text{RAMC}$$

Substituting again,

$$\tan (\text{OAHC} - \text{RAMC}) = \cos (\text{lat}) \times \tan A$$

Or, in general,

$$\text{OAHC} = \text{RAMC} + \arctan [\cos (\text{lat}) \times \tan A]$$

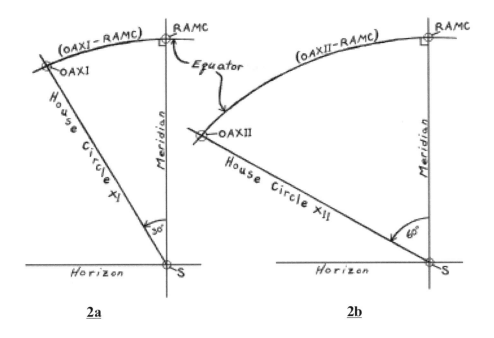

Basic arcs and angles for calculating OAHC and QHC of houses XI (2a) and XII (2b).

* * * * *

2c) Right spherical triangle referred to in derivations of equations for OAHC and QHC.

Figure 2: Campanus

Specifically,

$$OAXI = RAMC + \arctan[\cos(\text{lat}) \times \tan(30°)]$$

$$OAXII = RAMC + \arctan[\cos(\text{lat}) \times \tan(60°)]$$

From Figure 1b we see that OAII and OAIII will be easily measured in terms of RAIC (equal to RAMC + 180°) and will be numerically less than it. The derivation followed for the upper houses now yields these equations:

$$OAII = RAIC - \arctan[\cos(\text{lat}) \times \tan(60°)]$$

$$OAIII = RAIC - \arctan[\cos(\text{lat}) \times \tan(30°)]$$

In all cases 360° may be added or subtracted to facilitate calculations.

II. QHC

The same elements used to find OAHC can be used to find quasi-latitude (Figure 2c). First we solve for angle B, an analog of co-latitude for each house circle.

$$\cos B = \cos b \times \sin A$$

Since b = co-latitude,

$$\cos b = \cos(\text{co-lat}) = \sin(\text{lat})$$

Substituting, we have

$$\cos B = \sin(\text{lat}) \times \sin A$$

Since the use of a latitude analog will grant ready use of ascendant equations as a paradigm, we can modify the above equation to yield the complement of B, which we are calling Q (for "quasi-latitude").

$$\cos B = \cos(\text{co-Q}) = \sin Q$$

Thus, in general

$$\sin(QHC) = \sin(\text{lat}) \times \sin A$$

or

$$QHC = \arcsin[\sin(\text{lat}) \times \sin A]$$

Specifically,

$$QXI = \arcsin[\sin(\text{lat}) \times \sin(30°)]$$

$$QXII = \arcsin[\sin(\text{lat}) \times \sin(60°)]$$

A similar derivation for the lower houses yields

$$QII = \arcsin[\sin(\text{lat}) \times \sin(60°)]$$

$$QIII = \arcsin[\sin(\text{lat}) \times \sin(30°)]$$

III. Cusp longitudes

Having established parameters analogous to those used in computation of ascendants, we can use the same equations derived in *Ascendant Longitude Calculation* (page 21 *et seq*.). One need only substitute OAHC for RAEP, and QHC for latitude. Angle A between ecliptic and house circle must be calculated, as must critical values for OAHC (COAHC) in certain quadrants of the celestial equator. These equations are given in the summary below, but their derivation will not be repeated in this section.

Southern Hemisphere

Campanus equations for the southern hemisphere differ from northern only in calculation of the cusp longitude, and in the same way that Ascendant calculations differ from one hemisphere to the other.

Summary

The following summary of Campanus house system calculations is for latitudes less than (90° - OE); *i.e.*, all latitudes except the Arctic /Antarctic Circles and above.

I. OAHC
- A. OAXI = RAMC + arctan [cos (lat) × tan (30°)]
- B. OAXII = RAMC + arctan [cos (lat) × tan (60°)]
- C. OAII = RAIC - arctan [cos (lat) × tan (60°)]
- D. OAIII = RAIC - arctan [cos (lat) × tan (30°)]

II. QHC
- A. QXI = QIII = arcsin [sin (lat) × sin (30°)]
- B. QXII = QII = arcsin [sin (lat) × sin (60°)]

III. Cusps -- *Northern Hemisphere*
- A. 0° ≤ OAHC < 90°
  1) A = arccos [cos (OE) × sin (QHC) + sin (OE) × cos (QHC) × cos (OAHC)]
  2) COAHC = arccos [tan (OE) × tan (QHC)]

3) Cusp longitude

   a. OAHC < COAHC
   $$\text{cusp} = \arcsin\left[\frac{\cos(\text{QHC}) \times \sin(\text{OAHC})}{\sin A}\right]$$

   b. OAHC = COAHC
   cusp = 90°

   c. OAHC > COAHC
   $$\text{cusp} = 180° - \arcsin\left[\frac{\cos(\text{QHC}) \times \sin(\text{OAHC})}{\sin A}\right]$$

B. 90° ≤ OAHC < 180°

   1) A = arccos [- cos (OE) × sin (QHC) - sin (OE) × cos (QHC) × cos (OAHC)]

   2) $$\text{cusp} = 90° + \arccos\left[\frac{\cos(\text{QHC}) \times \cos(\text{OAHC} - 90°)}{\sin A}\right]$$

C. 180° ≤ OAHC < 270°

   1) A = arccos [- cos (OE) × sin (QHC) - sin (OE) × cos (QHC) × cos (OAHC)]

   2) $$\text{cusp} = 180° + \arcsin\left[\frac{\cos(\text{QHC}) \times \sin(\text{OAHC} - 180°)}{\sin A}\right]$$

D. 270° ≤ OAHC < 360°/0°

   1) A = arccos [cos (OE) × sin (QHC) + sin (OE) × cos (QHC) × cos (OAHC)]

   2) COAHC = 360° - arccos [tan (OE) × tan (QHC)]

   3) Cusp longitude

      a. OAHC < COAHC
      $$\text{cusp} = 270° - \arccos\left[\frac{\cos(\text{QHC}) \times \cos(\text{OAHC} - 270°)}{\sin A}\right]$$

      b. OAHC = COAHC
      cusp = 270°

      c. OAHC > COAHC
      $$\text{cusp} = 270° + \arccos\left[\frac{\cos(\text{QHC}) \times \cos(\text{OAHC} - 270°)}{\sin A}\right]$$

IV. Cusps -- *Southern Hemisphere*

    A. $0° \leq \text{OAHC} < 90°$

        1)   A = arccos [- cos (OE) × sin (QHC) + sin (OE) × cos (QHC) × cos (OAHC)]

        2) $\text{cusp} = \arcsin \left[\dfrac{\cos (\text{QHC}) \times \sin (\text{OAHC})}{\sin A} \right]$

    B. $90° \leq \text{OAHC} < 180°$

        1)   A = arccos [cos (OE) × sin (QHC) - sin (OE) × cos (QHC) × cos (OAHC)]

        2)   COAHC = arccos [- tan (OE) × tan (QHC)]

        3)   Cusp longitude

            a.   OAHC < COAHC

$$\text{cusp} = 90° - \arccos \left[\dfrac{\cos (\text{QHC}) \times \cos (\text{OAHC} - 90°)}{\sin A} \right]$$

            b.   OAHC = COAHC

cusp = 90°

            c.   OAHC > COAHC

$$\text{cusp} = 90° + \arccos \left[\dfrac{\cos (\text{QHC}) \times \cos (\text{OAHC} - 90°)}{\sin A} \right]$$

    C. $180° \leq \text{OAHC} < 270°$

        1)   A = arccos [cos (OE) × sin (QHC) - sin (OE) × cos (QHC) × cos (OAHC)]

        2)   COAHC = 360° - arccos [- tan (OE) × tan (QHC)]

        3)   Cusp longitude

            a.   OAHC < COAHC

$$\text{cusp} = 180° + \arcsin \left[\dfrac{\cos (\text{QHC}) \times \sin (\text{OAHC} - 180°)}{\sin A} \right]$$

            b.   OAHC = COAHC

cusp = 270°

            c.   OAHC > COAHC

$$\text{cusp} = 360° - \arcsin \left[\dfrac{\cos (\text{QHC}) \times \sin (\text{OAHC} - 180°)}{\sin A} \right]$$

D. $270° \leq \text{OAHC} < 360°/0°$

1) $A = \arccos[-\cos(\text{OE}) \times \sin(\text{QHC}) + \sin(\text{OE}) \times \cos(\text{QHC}) \times \cos(\text{OAHC})]$

2) $\text{cusp} = 270° + \arccos\left[\dfrac{\cos(\text{QHC}) \times \cos(\text{OAHC} - 270°)}{\sin A}\right]$

Campanus at Circumpolar Latitudes

[Latitude ≥ (90° - OE)]

Applicability of the previously established equations beyond the Arctic/ Antarctic Circles diminishes as latitude increases. The trouble occurs during those sidereal time - latitude conditions for which the ecliptic falls below the southern horizon (or northern horizon in the Antarctic). It is necessary, therefore, to calculate the span of sidereal time during which this horizon - ecliptic configuration obtains for a given latitude. (See *Arctic Region Asc Calculations*, p. 33 *et seq.*) The end points of this sidereal time period I have called "points of critical ecliptic declination" (PCED's); their calculation is included in the summary of equations below.

When the RAMC falls outside the PCED's, the lower latitude house cusp equations are effective. However, an RAMC within the PCED's for a given latitude (the "twilight zone") creates the situation seen in Figures 3a and b: the ecliptic does not cross the quadrants in which we usually expect to find the house cusps we are calculating. Since the MC lies below the horizon, so also must cusps XI and XII. Similarly, II and III must fall above the northern horizon, where we find the IC. To complicate matters, the equator, as always (except at the exact poles), lies above the southern horizon and below the northern horizon. In order to project the house circles from the trisected prime vertical through the equator (to find OAHC) and onto the ecliptic (to find longitude), we must divide the quadrant of the prime vertical "next door" to the one usually divided. The house circles will then extend from the prime vertical through the equator, and through the south (or north) point of the horizon before intersecting the ecliptic. Deriving house cusp equations for a "twilight zone" RAMC thus becomes more devious, but not less possible, than deriving them for lower latitudes. In their final form, these equations closely resemble standard equations for the opposite hemisphere, with this difference: OAHC's are seen to decrease numerically as house cusps increase in longitude.

The same problems are encountered in the Antarctic region as in the Arctic. The only difference is in the arc of the ecliptic which falls below the horizon during the critical sidereal period.

One may expect to find extreme differences in house sizes in the problematical circumpolar latitudes. It is visually obvious from Figures 3a and b that the occasional multiple sign interceptions are perfectly in line with the geometry of the Campanus system.

For brevity, the derivations of these equations have not been included, but a complete summary of them follows.

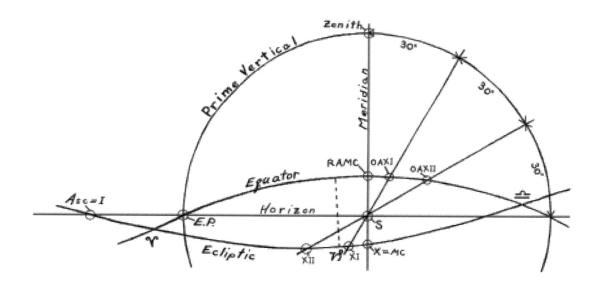

3a) "Upper" houses, with cusps now below the horizon.

* * * * *

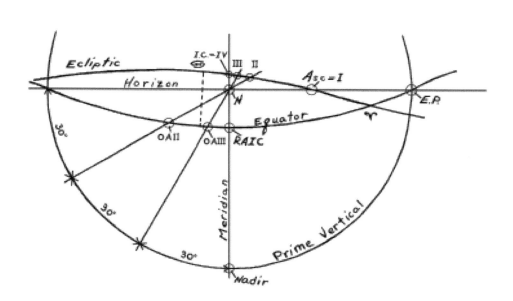

3b) "Lower" houses, with cusps now above the horizon.

* * * * *

Figure 3:
Campanus at Circumpolar Latitudes

❧ Summary ❧

Latitude ≥ (90° - OE) North

I. PCED's (These should have been determined during calculation of the Asc, unless another source was used to determine it)

    A. Declination of horizon $(decl_h) = 90° - lat$

    B. PCED's

        1) $PCED1 = 180° + \arcsin \left[\dfrac{\tan(decl_h)}{\tan(OE)} \right]$

        2) $PCED2 = 360° - \arcsin \left[\dfrac{\tan(decl_h)}{\tan(OE)} \right]$

II. PCED1 > RAMC > PCED2

    Proceed with equations for lower latitudes.

III. PCED1 ≤ RAMC ≤ PCED2

    A. OAHC

        1) $OAXI = RAMC - \arctan[\cos(lat) \times \tan(30°)]$

        2) $OAXII = RAMC - \arctan[\cos(lat) \times \tan(60°)]$

        3) $OAII = RAIC + \arctan[\cos(lat) \times \tan(60°)]$

        4) $OAIII = RAIC + \arctan[\cos(lat) \times \tan(30°)]$

    B. QHC: as for lower latitudes

    C. Cusps

        1) $0° \leq OAHC < 90°$

            a. $A = \arccos[-\cos(OE) \times \sin(QHC) + \sin(OE) \times \cos(QHC) \times \cos OAHC]$

            b. $cusp = \arcsin \left[\dfrac{\cos(QHC) \times \sin(OAHC)}{\sin A} \right]$

        2) $90° \leq OAHC < 180°$

            a. $A = \arccos[\cos(OE) \times \sin(QHC) - \sin(OE) \times \cos(QHC) \times \cos(OAHC)]$

            b. $COAHC = \arccos[-\tan(OE) \times \tan(QHC)]$

            c. Cusp longitude

                i. OAHC < COAHC

$$cusp = 90° - \arccos \left[\dfrac{\cos(QHC) \times \cos(OAHC - 90°)}{\sin A} \right]$$

ii. OAHC = COAHC

cusp = 90°

iii. OAHC > COAHC

$$\text{cusp} = 90° + \arccos\left[\frac{\cos(QHC) \times \cos(OAHC - 90°)}{\sin A}\right]$$

3) 180° ≤ OAHC < 270°

a. A = arccos [cos (OE) × sin (QHC) −
sin (OE) × cos (QHC) × cos (OAHC)]

b. COAHC = 360° − arccos [− tan (OE) × tan (QHC)]

c. Cusp longitude

i. OAHC < COAHC

$$\text{cusp} = 180° + \arcsin\left[\frac{\cos(QHC) \times \sin(OAHC - 180°)}{\sin A}\right]$$

ii. OAHC = COAHC

cusp = 270°

iii. OAHC > COAHC

$$\text{cusp} = 360° - \arcsin\left[\frac{\cos(QHC) \times \sin(OAHC - 180°)}{\sin A}\right]$$

4) 270° ≤ OAHC < 360°/0°

a. A = arccos [− cos (OE) × sin (QHC) +
sin(OE) × cos (QHC) × cos (OAHC)]

b. $\text{cusp} = 270° + \arccos\left[\frac{\cos(QHC) \times \cos(OAHC - 270°)}{\sin A}\right]$

Points of Failure:

1) At sidereal Time = $18^h\ 00^m\ 00^s$, latitude = (90° − OE)

2) At exact North Pole

3) At RAMC = PCED1 or PCED2, when Asc will be opposite MC

$$\text{Latitude} \geq (90° - OE) \text{ South}$$

I. PCED calculation (if not done previously)

  A. $\text{Decl}_h = 90° - \text{lat}$

  B. PCED's

  1) $\text{PCED1} = \arcsin\left[\dfrac{\tan(\text{decl}_h)}{\tan(\text{OE})}\right]$

  2) $\text{PCED2} = 180° - \arcsin\left[\dfrac{\tan(\text{decl}_h)}{\tan(\text{OE})}\right]$

II. PCED1 > RAMC > PCED2

  Proceed with equations for lower south latitudes.

III. PCED1 ≤ RAMC ≤ PCED2

  A. OAHC: calculated as for north circumpolar region

  B. QHC: calculated as for north circumpolar region

  C. Cusps

  1) $0° \leq \text{OAHC} < 90°$

    a. $A = \arccos[\cos(\text{OE}) \times \sin(\text{QHC}) + \sin(\text{OE}) \times \cos(\text{QHC}) \times \cos(\text{OAHC})]$

    b. $\text{COAHC} = \arccos[\tan(\text{OE}) \times \tan(\text{QHC})]$

    c. Cusp longitude

      i. OAHC < COAHC

      $$\text{cusp} = \arcsin\left[\dfrac{\cos(\text{QHC}) \times \sin(\text{OAHC})}{\sin A}\right]$$

      ii. OAHC = COAHC

      cusp = 90°

      iii. OAHC > COAHC

      $$\text{cusp} = 180° - \arcsin\left[\dfrac{\cos(\text{QHC}) \times \sin(\text{OAHC})}{\sin A}\right]$$

  2) $90° \leq \text{OAHC} < 180°$

    a. $A = \arccos[-\cos(\text{OE}) \times \sin(\text{QHC}) - \sin(\text{OE}) \times \cos(\text{QHC}) \times \cos(\text{OAHC})]$

    b. $\text{cusp} = 90° + \arccos\left[\dfrac{\cos(\text{QHC}) \times \cos(\text{OAHC} - 90°)}{\sin A}\right]$

3) $180° \leq \text{OAHC} < 270°$

    a. $A = \arccos[-\cos(\text{OE}) \times \sin(\text{QHC}) - \sin(\text{OE}) \times \cos(\text{QHC}) \times \cos(\text{OAHC})]$

    b. $\text{cusp} = 180° + \arcsin\left[\dfrac{\cos(\text{QHC}) \times \sin(\text{OAHC} - 180°)}{\sin A}\right]$

4) $270° \leq \text{OAHC} < 360°/0°$

    a. $A = \arccos[\cos(\text{OE}) \times \sin(\text{QHC}) + \sin(\text{OE}) \times \cos(\text{QHC}) \times \cos(\text{OAHC})]$

    b. $\text{COAHC} = 360° - \arccos[\tan(\text{OE}) \times \tan(\text{QHC})]$

    c. Cusp longitude

        i. $\text{OAHC} < \text{COAHC}$

$$\text{cusp} = 270° - \arccos\left[\dfrac{\cos(\text{QHC}) \times \cos(\text{OAHC} - 270°)}{\sin A}\right]$$

        ii. $\text{OAHC} = \text{COAHC}$

            $\text{cusp} = 270°$

        iii. $\text{OAHC} > \text{COAHC}$

$$\text{cusp} = 270° + \arccos\left[\dfrac{\cos(\text{QHC}) \times \cos(\text{OAHC} - 270°)}{\sin A}\right]$$

Points of Failure:

1) At Sidereal Time = $6^h\,00^m\,00^s$, latitude = $(90° - \text{OE})$
2) At exact South Pole
3) At RAMC = PCED1 or PCED2, when Asc will be opposite MC

❧ Examples ❦

1) April 4, 1949; ST = $3^h 42^m 25^s$; OE = 23.448333°;
geocentric latitude = 39.560115° N; RAMC = 55.604167°; MC = 57.868217°;
Asc = 152.5121°

I. OAHC

$$OAXI = 55.604167° + 23.994425° = 79.598592°$$
$$OAXII = 55.604167° + 53.171377° = 108.77554°$$
$$OAII = 235.60417° - 53.171377° = 182.77554°$$
$$OAIII = 235.60417° - 23.994425° = 211.60974°$$

II. QHC

$$QXI = QIII = 18.568834°$$
$$QXII = QII = 33.474151°$$

III. Cusp longitudes

XI
A = 68.884537°
COAXI = 81.621765°; OAXI < COAXI
cusp = 88.138926°

XII
A = 113.52693°
cusp = 120.53156°

II
A = 100.04322°
cusp = 182.06068°

III
A = 88.332618°
cusp = 209.80541°

IV. Summary

X/MC	= 27° ♉ 52' 06"	IV/IC	= 27° ♏ 52' 06"
XI	= 28° ♊ 08' 20"	V	= 28° ♐ 08' 20"
XII	= 0° ♌ 31' 54"	VI	= 0° ♒ 31' 54"
I/Asc	= 2° ♍ 30' 44"	VII/Desc	= 2° ♓ 30' 44"
II	= 2° ♎ 03' 38"	VIII	= 2° ♈ 03' 38"
III	= 29° ♎ 48' 19"	IX	= 29° ♈ 48' 19"

♋ and ♑ intercepted

2) January 14, 1935; ST = $10^h 33^m 14^s$; OE = 23.448889°;
geocentric latitude = 52.213013° **S**; RAMC = 158.30833°; MC = 156.559047°;
Asc = 280.61609°

    I.   OAHC

        OAXI = 177.78999°
        OAXII = 205.01105°
        OAII = 291.60561°
        OAIII = 318.82667°

    II.   QHC

        QXI = QIII = 23.275148°
        QXII = QII = 43.189606°

    III.   Cusp longitudes

    XI
        A = 43.298683°
        COAXI = 100.75327°; OAXI > COAXI
        cusp = 177.03915°

    XII
        A = 27.024185°
        COAXII = 245.97268°; OAXII < COAXII
        cusp = 222.72099°

    II
        A = 121.40358°
        cusp = 307.41993°

    III
        A = 95.724625°
        cusp = 322.56989°

    IV.   Summary

X/MC	= 6° ♍ 33' 33"		IV/IC	= 6° ♓ 33' 33"
XI	= 27° ♍ 02' 21"		V	= 27° ♓ 02' 21"
XII	= 12° ♏ 43' 16"		VI	= 12° ♉ 43' 16"
I/Asc	= 10° ♑ 36' 58"		VII/Desc	= 10° ♋ 36' 58"
II	= 7° ♒ 25' 12"		VIII	= 7° ♌ 25' 12"
III	= 22° ♒ 34' 12"		IX	= 22° ♌ 34' 12"

♈, ♊, ♎ and ♐ intercepted

3) July 12, 1978; ST = $12^h 22^m 38^s$; OE = 23.439444°;
geocentric latitude = 21.41829° **N**; RAMC = 185.65833°; MC = 186.16349°;
Asc = 266.2291°

I. OAHC

$\quad$ OAXI = 213.91538°
$\quad$ OAXII = 243.85195°
$\quad$ OAII = 307.46471°
$\quad$ OAIII = 337.40128°

II. QHC

$\quad$ QXI = QIII = 10.520481°
$\quad$ QXII = QII = 18.436288°

III. Cusp longitudes

XI
$\quad$ A = 80.965267°
$\quad$ cusp = 213.74378°

XII
$\quad$ A = 97.114465°
$\quad$ cusp = 239.11444°

II
$\quad$ A = 58.688308°
$\quad$ COAII = 278.31006°; OAII > COAII
$\quad$ cusp = 298.19337°

III
$\quad$ A = 58.090147°
$\quad$ COAIII = 274.61818°; OAIII > COAIII
$\quad$ cusp = 333.57192°

IV. Summary

X/MC	= 6° ♎ 09' 49"		IV/IC	= 6° ♈ 09' 49"
XI	= 3° ♏ 44' 38"		V	= 3° ♉ 44' 38"
XII	= 29° ♏ 06' 52"		VI	= 29° ♉ 06' 52"
I/Asc	= 26° ♐ 13' 45"		VII/Desc	= 26° ♊ 13' 45"
II	= 28° ♑ 11' 36"		VIII	= 28° ♋ 11' 36"
III	= 3° ♓ 34' 19"		IX	= 3° ♍ 34' 19"

♌ and ♒ intercepted

4) November 23, 1918; ST = $22^h 47^m 07^s$; OE = 23.450278°;
geocentric latitude = 40.092814° **S**; RAMC = 341.779167°; MC = 40.260849°;
Asc = 56.78703°

    I.   OAHC

           OAXI = 5.60897°
           OAXII = 34.73716°
           OAII = 108.82116°
           OAIII = 137.94935°

    II.   QHC

           QXI = QIII = 18.784757°
           QXII = QII = 33.899947°

    III.   Cusp longitudes

        XI

           A = 85.438169°
           cusp = 5.326247°

        XII

           A = 103.90074°
           cusp = 29.158078°

        II

           A = 51.812299°
           COAII = 106.94707°; OAII > COAII
           cusp = 91.728053°

        III

           A = 54.88785°
           COAIII = 98.484526°; OAIII > COAIII
           cusp = 129.1795°

    IV.   Summary

X/MC	= 10° ♓ 15' 39"	IV/IC	= 10° ♍ 15' 39"
XI	= 5° ♈ 19' 34"	V	= 5° ♎ 19' 34"
XII	= 29° ♈ 09' 29"	VI	= 29° ♎ 09' 29"
I/Asc	= 26° ♉ 47' 13"	VII/Desc	= 26° ♏ 47' 13"
II	= 1° ♋ 43' 41"	VIII	= 1° ♑ 43' 41"
III	= 9° ♌ 10' 46"	IX	= 9° ♒ 10' 46"

♊ and ♐ intercepted

5) March 15, 1964; ST = $16^h 13^m 06^s$; OE = 23.44375°;
geocentric latitude = 72.740801° **N**; RAMC = 243.275°; MC = 245.2063°;
Asc = 44.282764°; ⇨Note lat > (90° - OE)

- I. PCED's
  - PCED1 = 225.76196°
  - PCED2 = 314.23804°
  - RAMC falls within "twilight zone": special polar equations must be used.
- II. OAHC
  - OAXI = 233.55475°
  - OAXII = 216.07679°
  - OAII = 90.473208°
  - OAIII = 72.995249°
- III. QHC
  - QXI = QIII = 28.521348°
  - QXII = QII = 55.794875°
- IV. Cusp longitudes
  - XI
    - A = 49.779491°
    - COAXI = 256.3695°; OAXI < COAXI
    - cusp = 247.76765°
  - XII
    - A = 20.028399°
    - COAXII = 230.35959°; OAXII < COAXII
    - cusp = 255.14358°
  - II
    - A = 40.482261°
    - COAII = 129.66406°; OAII < COAII
    - cusp = 59.982986°
  - III
    - A = 109.62359°
    - cusp = 63.13018°
- V. Summary

X/MC	=	5° ♐ 12' 23"	IV/IC	=	5° ♊ 12' 23"
XI	=	7° ♐ 46' 04"	V	=	7° ♊ 46' 04"
XII	=	15° ♐ 08' 37"	VI	=	15° ♊ 08' 37"
I/Asc	=	14° ♉ 16' 58"	VII/Desc	=	14° ♏ 16' 58"
II	=	29° ♉ 58' 59"	VIII	=	29° ♏ 58' 59"
III	=	3° ♊ 07' 49"	IX	=	3° ♐ 07' 49"

♈, ♋, ♌, ♍, ♎, ♑, ♒ and ♓ intercepted (!)

4a) Looking SE, above the horizon, where houses X, XI and XII are measured.

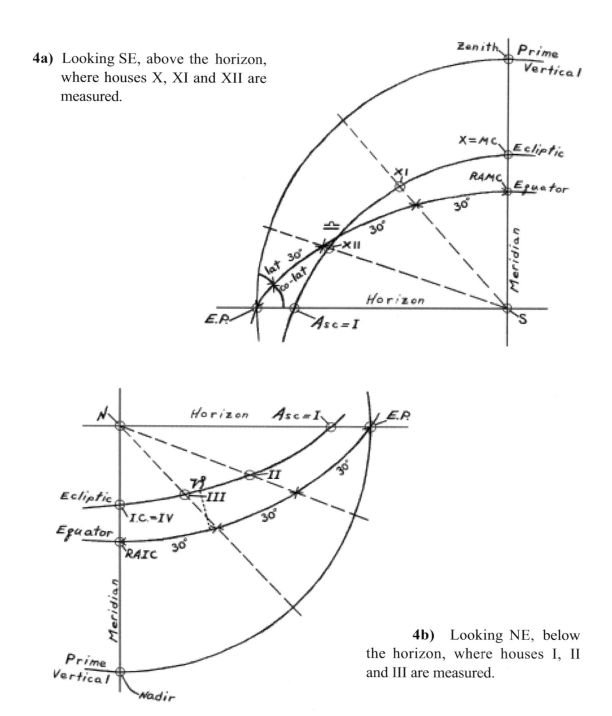

4b) Looking NE, below the horizon, where houses I, II and III are measured.

Figure 4: Regiomontanus

Regiomontanus

The basis for house division by Regiomontanus is the trisection of quadrant arcs of the celestial equator between meridian and horizon. The house circles intersect the prime vertical at right angles and pass through the north and south points of the horizon; intersections with the ecliptic mark cusp longitudes. The lunes of the celestial sphere so derived are unequal in size, except at the equator (Figures 4a and b, facing page).

In comparing Regiomontanus to the previously "dissected" system, one will find a good deal of similarity to the geometry of Campanus, with this basic difference: Regiomontanus departs from the strictly mundane geodetic "target" of Campanus with the introduction of a celestial element (the equator) into the derivation of the intermediate house circles. Thus we have a blending of two co-ordinate systems: the equatorial, which provides the angular separation of the house circles; and the horizontal (comprising the prime vertical and meridian), which provides a north-south axis in the plane of the horizon about which the houses are clustered.

Regiomontanus suggests to me that the alignment of cosmic influences (as represented by the zodiac) with the fields of human experiences (the houses) is more than just a matter of geography. Rather, the clockwork of our geocentric universe (sidereal time, measured as right ascension along the equator) determines the "time" of the zodiac allotted to the houses of the horoscope.

In Regiomontanus as in Campanus, the house circle is treated as a quasi-horizon; its intersection with the ecliptic, the house cusp, is then a quasi-Ascendant calculated from the oblique ascension of the house cusp and the quasi-latitude of the house circle. Since house division is based on direct trisection of the equator, computation of the former parameter is a simple arithmetic operation of adding multiples of 30° to the RAMC. Quasi-latitude is found using the laws of right spherical triangles. Actual computation of house cusps follows the paradigm established for Campanus. These operations are set out below.

Calculations

I.   OAHC (Figures 5a and b)

As noted above, calculation of this parameter is a simple arithmetic operation. The equatorial quadrant from RAMC to East Point (90°) is trisected, as is the quadrant from East Point to RAIC (90°). Thus, intermediate house circles are established by addition of multiples of 30° to the RAMC.

$$OAXI = RAMC + 30°$$
$$OAXII = RAMC + 60°$$
$$OAII = RAMC + 120° \text{ or } RAIC - 60°$$
$$OAIII = RAMC + 150° \text{ or } RAIC - 30°$$

In all cases 360° may be added or subtracted to facilitate calculations.

II.   QHC (Figure 5c)

The operation here is the solution of a spherical right triangle for an unknown angle. Two sides are known: a, equal to 30° or 60° (see Figures 5a and b); and b, which is subtended by the angle of geocentric co-latitude at the East Point and is equal to it (see Figures 4a and b). To reiterate:

In triangle ABC, B = complement of QHC; C = 90°; a = 30° for XI and III, and 60° for XII and II; b = geocentric co-latitude.

In a right spherical triangle

$$\tan B = \frac{\tan b}{\sin a}$$

Substituting,

$$\tan B = \frac{\tan (\text{co-lat})}{\sin a}$$

It would be more convenient to work from latitude than from co-latitude, its complement; therefore

$$\tan B = \frac{1}{\tan (\text{lat}) \times \sin a}$$

Likewise, since the Asc calculation paradigm we will employ uses quasi-latitude rather than quasi-co-latitude, we can modify the above equation to solve for the complement of B, which complement we are calling Q(HC). Thus, this general equation:

$$\tan Q = \tan (\text{lat}) \times \sin a$$

Specifically,

$$QXI = QIII = \arctan [\tan (\text{lat}) \times \sin (30°)]$$

$$QXII = QII = \arctan [\tan (\text{lat}) \times \sin (60°)]$$

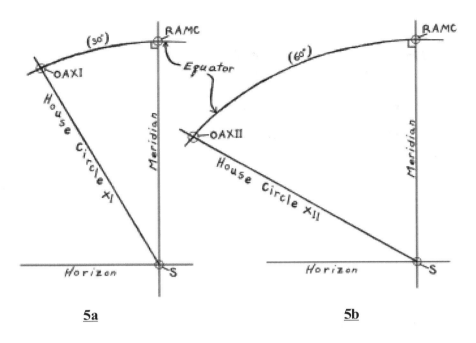

Basic arcs and angles for calculating OAHC and QHC of houses XI (5a) and XII (5b).

* * * * *

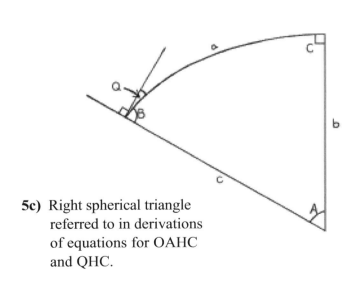

5c) Right spherical triangle referred to in derivations of equations for OAHC and QHC.

Figure 5: Regiomontanus

III. Cusp longitude

As with Campanus, the cusps are computed using as paradigm the equations for calculation of ascendants. One merely substitutes OAHC for RAEP, and QHC for latitude. These equations are given in the summary below.

∾ Southern Hemisphere ∽

Regiomontanus equations differ from northern to southern hemisphere in the same way as do Asc equations. The equations are given in the summary below.

∾ Summary ∽

Latitude < (90° - OE)

I. OAHC

    A. OAXI = RAMC + 30°
    B. OAXII = RAMC + 60°
    C. OAII = RAMC + 120° <u>or</u> RAIC - 60°
    D. OAIII = RAMC + 150° <u>or</u> RAIC - 30°

(Subtract 360° from results when necessary)

II. QHC

$$QXI = QIII = \arctan[\tan(lat) \times \sin(30°)]$$
$$QXII = QII = \arctan[\tan(lat) \times \sin(60°)]$$

III. Cusps -- *Northern Hemisphere*

    A. 0° ≤ OAHC < 90°

        1) $A = \arccos[\cos(OE) \times \sin(QHC) + \sin(OE) \times \cos(QHC) \times \cos(OAHC)]$

        2) $COAHC = \arccos[\tan(OE) \times \tan(QHC)]$

        3) Cusp longitude

            a. OAHC < COAHC
$$cusp = \arcsin\left[\frac{\cos(QHC) \times \sin(OAHC)}{\sin A}\right]$$

            b. OAHC = COAHC
               cusp = 90°

            c. OAHC > COAHC
$$cusp = 180° - \arcsin\left[\frac{\cos(QHC) \times \sin(OAHC)}{\sin A}\right]$$

B. $90° \leq OAHC < 180°$

1) $A = \arccos[-\cos(OE) \times \sin(QHC) - \sin(OE) \times \cos(QHC) \times \cos(OAHC)]$

2) $cusp = 90° + \arccos\left[\dfrac{\cos(QHC) \times \cos(OAHC - 90°)}{\sin A}\right]$

C. $180° \leq OAHC < 270°$

1) $A = \arccos[-\cos(OE) \times \sin(QHC) - \sin(OE) \times \cos(QHC) \times \cos(OAHC)]$

2) $cusp = 180° + \arcsin\left[\dfrac{\cos(QHC) \times \sin(OAHC - 180°)}{\sin A}\right]$

D. $270° \leq OAHC < 360°/0°$

1) $A = \arccos[\cos(OE) \times \sin(QHC) + \sin(OE) \times \cos(QHC) \times \cos(OAHC)]$

2) $COAHC = 360° - \arccos[\tan(OE) \times \tan(QHC)]$

3) Cusp longitude

a. $OAHC < COAHC$

$cusp = 270° - \arccos\left[\dfrac{\cos(QHC) \times \cos(OAHC - 270°)}{\sin A}\right]$

b. $OAHC = COAHC$

$cusp = 270°$

c. $OAHC > COAHC$

$cusp = 270° + \arccos\left[\dfrac{\cos(QHC) \times \cos(OAHC - 270°)}{\sin A}\right]$

IV. Cusps -- *Southern Hemisphere*

A. $0° \leq OAHC < 90°$

1) $A = \arccos[-\cos(OE) \times \sin(QHC) + \sin(OE) \times \cos(QHC) \times \cos(OAHC)]$

2) $cusp = \arcsin\left[\dfrac{\cos(QHC) \times \sin(OAHC)}{\sin A}\right]$

B. $90° \leq OAHC < 180°$

1) $A = \arccos[\cos(OE) \times \sin(QHC) - \sin(OE) \times \cos(QHC) \times \cos(OAHC)]$

2) $COAHC = \arccos[-\tan(OE) \times \tan(QHC)]$

3) Cusp longitude

    a. OAHC < COAHC

$$\text{cusp} = 90° - \arccos\left[\frac{\cos(\text{QHC}) \times \cos(\text{OAHC} - 90°)}{\sin A}\right]$$

    b. OAHC = COAHC

    cusp = 90°

    c. OAHC > COAHC

$$\text{cusp} = 90° + \arccos\left[\frac{\cos(\text{QHC}) \times \cos(\text{OAHC} - 90°)}{\sin A}\right]$$

C. $180° \leq \text{OAHC} < 270°$

1) A = arccos [cos (OE) × sin (QHC) −
    sin (OE) × cos (QHC) × cos (OAHC)]

2) COAHC = 360° − arccos [− tan (OE) × tan (QHC)]

3) Cusp longitude

    a. OAHC < COAHC

$$\text{cusp} = 180° + \arcsin\left[\frac{\cos(\text{QHC}) \times \sin(\text{OAHC} - 180°)}{\sin A}\right]$$

    b. OAHC = COAHC

    cusp = 270°

    c. OAHC > COAHC

$$\text{cusp} = 360° - \arcsin\left[\frac{\cos(\text{QHC}) \times \sin(\text{OAHC} - 180°)}{\sin A}\right]$$

D. $270° \leq \text{OAHC} < 360°/0°$

1) A = arccos [− cos (OE) × sin (QHC) +
    sin (OE) × cos (QHC) × cos (OAHC)]

2) $\text{cusp} = 270° + \arccos\left[\dfrac{\cos(\text{QHC}) \times \cos(\text{OAHC} - 270°)}{\sin A}\right]$

Regiomontanus at Circumpolar Latitudes

[Latitude ≥ (90° - OE)]

At these high latitudes Regiomontanus calculations are party to the same complications as are those for Campanus houses. The problem is solved in the same way: by division of an equatorial arc lying in a celestial quadrant other than that of the ecliptic arc ultimately to be divided (Figures 6a and b). As with those other calculations, this technique is employed when the MC falls below the horizon and the IC lies above the horizon. Some extreme cases of sign interception may be expected, although houses would tend to be less disparate in size than those of Campanus for the same birth data. The summary includes equations for both north and south circumpolar latitudes.

❧ *Summary* ❧

Latitude ≥ (90° - OE) North

I. PCED's (These should have been determined during calculation of the Asc, unless another source was used to determine it)

   A. Declination of horizon $(decl_h) = 90° - lat$

   B. PCED's

   1) $PCED1 = 180° + \arcsin\left[\dfrac{\tan(decl_h)}{\tan(OE)}\right]$

   2) $PCED2 = 360° - \arcsin\left[\dfrac{\tan(decl_h)}{\tan(OE)}\right]$

II. PCED1 > RAMC > PCED2

   Proceed with equations for lower latitudes.

III. PCED1 ≤ RAMC ≤ PCED2

   A. OAHC

   1) OAXI = RAMC - 30°
   2) OAXII = RAMC - 60°
   3) OAII = RAMC - 120° *or* RAIC + 60°
   4) OAIII = RAMC - 150° *or* RAIC + 30°

   B. QHC: as for lower latitudes.

   ⇨ Note if QHC > (90° - OE).

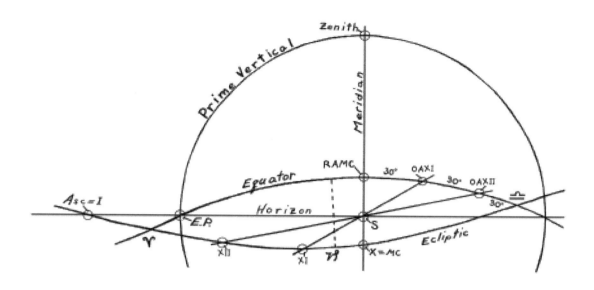

6a) "Upper" houses, with cusps now below the horizon.

* * * * *

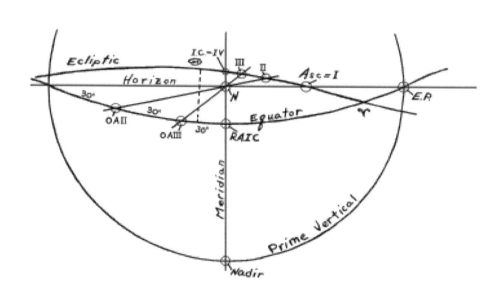

6b) "Lower" houses, with cusps now above the horizon.

* * * * *

Figure 6:
Regiomontanus at Circumpolar Latitudes

C. Cusps

1) $0° \leq OAHC < 90°$

   a. $A = \arccos[-\cos(OE) \times \sin(QHC) + \sin(OE) \times \cos(QHC) \times \cos OAHC)]$

   b. $\text{cusp} = \arcsin\left[\dfrac{\cos(QHC) \times \sin(OAHC)}{\sin A}\right]$

2) $90° \leq OAHC < 180°$

   a. $A = \arccos[\cos(OE) \times \sin(QHC) - \sin(OE) \times \cos(QHC) \times \cos(OAHC)]$

   b. $COAHC = \arccos[-\tan(OE) \times \tan(QHC)]$

   ⇨ If $QHC > (90° - OE)$, then COAHC is undefined.

   c. Cusp longitude

   i. OAHC < COAHC; or COAHC undefined

   $\text{cusp} = 90° - \arccos\left[\dfrac{\cos(QHC) \times \cos(OAHC - 90°)}{\sin A}\right]$

   ii. OAHC = COAHC
   cusp = 90°

   iii. OAHC > COAHC

   $\text{cusp} = 90° + \arccos\left[\dfrac{\cos(QHC) \times \cos(OAHC - 90°)}{\sin A}\right]$

3) $180° \leq OAHC < 270°$

   a. $A = \arccos[\cos(OE) \times \sin(QHC) - \sin(OE) \times \cos(QHC) \times \cos(OAHC)]$

   b. $COAHC = 360° - \arccos[-\tan(OE) \times \tan(QHC)]$

   ⇨ If $QHC > (90° - OE)$, then COAHC is undefined.

   c. Cusp longitude

   i. OAHC < COAHC

   $\text{cusp} = 180° + \arcsin\left[\dfrac{\cos(QHC) \times \sin(OAHC - 180°)}{\sin A}\right]$

   ii. OAHC = COAHC
   cusp = 270°

iii. OAHC > COAHC; or COAHC undefined

$$\text{cusp} = 360° - \arcsin\left[\frac{\cos(QHC) \times \sin(OAHC - 180°)}{\sin A}\right]$$

4) $270° \leq OAHC < 360°/0°$

    a. $A = \arccos[-\cos(OE) \times \sin(QHC) + \sin(OE) \times \cos(QHC) \times \cos(OAHC)]$

    b. $\text{cusp} = 270° + \arccos\left[\dfrac{\cos(QHC) \times \cos(OAHC - 270°)}{\sin A}\right]$

Points of Failure:

1) At sidereal Time = $18^h\ 00^m\ 00^s$, latitude = $(90° - OE)$
2) At exact North Pole
3) At RAMC = PCED1 or PCED2, when Asc will be opposite MC

⌘

Latitude ≥ (90° - OE) South

I. PCED calculation (if not done previously)

    A. $\text{Decl}_h = 90° - \text{lat}$

    B. PCED's

        1) $\text{PCED1} = \arcsin\left[\dfrac{\tan(\text{decl}_h)}{\tan(OE)}\right]$

        2) $\text{PCED2} = 180° - \arcsin\left[\dfrac{\tan(\text{decl}_h)}{\tan(OE)}\right]$

II. PCED1 > RAMC > PCED2

Proceed with equations for lower south latitudes.

III. PCED1 ≤ RAMC ≤ PCED2

    A. OAHC: calculated as for north circumpolar region

    B. QHC: calculated as for north circumpolar region

        ⇨ Note if QHC > (90° - OE).

C. Cusps

    1) $0° \leq \text{OAHC} < 90°$

        a. $A = \arccos[\cos(\text{OE}) \times \sin(\text{QHC}) + \sin(\text{OE}) \times \cos(\text{QHC}) \times \cos(\text{OAHC})]$

        b. $\text{COAHC} = \arccos[\tan(\text{OE}) \times \tan(\text{QHC})]$

            ⇨ If $\text{QHC} > (90° - \text{OE})$, then COAHC is undefined.

        c. Cusp longitude

            i. OAHC < COAHC

$$\text{cusp} = \arcsin\left[\frac{\cos(\text{QHC}) \times \sin(\text{OAHC})}{\sin A}\right]$$

            ii. OAHC = COAHC

                cusp = 90°

            iii. OAHC > COAHC; or COAHC undefined

$$\text{cusp} = 180° - \arcsin\left[\frac{\cos(\text{QHC}) \times \sin(\text{OAHC})}{\sin A}\right]$$

    2) $90° \leq \text{OAHC} < 180°$

        a. $A = \arccos[-\cos(\text{OE}) \times \sin(\text{QHC}) - \sin(\text{OE}) \times \cos(\text{QHC}) \times \cos(\text{OAHC})]$

        b. $\text{cusp} = 90° + \arccos\left[\dfrac{\cos(\text{QHC}) \times \cos(\text{OAHC} - 90°)}{\sin A}\right]$

    3) $180° \leq \text{OAHC} < 270°$

        a. $A = \arccos[-\cos(\text{OE}) \times \sin(\text{QHC}) - \sin(\text{OE}) \times \cos(\text{QHC}) \times \cos(\text{OAHC})]$

        b. $\text{cusp} = 180° + \arcsin\left[\dfrac{\cos(\text{QHC}) \times \sin(\text{OAHC} - 180°)}{\sin A}\right]$

    4) $270° \leq \text{OAHC} < 360°/0°$

        a. $A = \arccos[\cos(\text{OE}) \times \sin(\text{QHC}) + \sin(\text{OE}) \times \cos(\text{QHC}) \times \cos(\text{OAHC})]$

        b. $\text{COAHC} = 360° - \arccos[\tan(\text{OE}) \times \tan(\text{QHC})]$

            ⇨ If $\text{QHC} > (90° - \text{OE})$, then COAHC is undefined.

  c. Cusp longitude

    i. OAHC < COAHC; or COAHC undefined

$$\text{cusp} = 270° - \arccos\left[\frac{\cos(\text{QHC}) \times \cos(\text{OAHC} - 270°)}{\sin A}\right]$$

    ii. OAHC = COAHC

     cusp = 270°

    iii. OAHC > COAHC

$$\text{cusp} = 270° + \arccos\left[\frac{\cos(\text{QHC}) \times \cos(\text{OAHC} - 270°)}{\sin A}\right]$$

Points of Failure:

1) At Sidereal Time = $6^h\,00^m\,00^s$, latitude = (90° - OE)
2) At exact South Pole
3) At RAMC = PCED1 or PCED2, when Asc will be opposite MC

❧ Examples ❦

1) April 4, 1949; ST = $3^h 42^m 25^s$; OE = 23.448333°;
geocentric latitude = 39.560115° **N**; RAMC = 55.604167°; MC = 57.868217°;
Asc = 152.5121°

I. OAHC

OAXI = 85.604167°
OAXII = 115.60417°
OAII = 175.60417°
OAIII = 205.60417°

II. QHC

QXI = QIII = 22.443075°
QXII = QII = 35.580827°

III. Cusp longitudes

XI

A = 67.763646°
COAXI = 79.67365°; OAXI > COAXI
cusp = 95.38832°

XII

A = 113.20018°
cusp = 127.06442°

II

A = 102.18829°
cusp = 176.34355°

III

A = 91.064143°
cusp = 203.54622°

IV. Summary

X/MC	= 27° ♉ 52' 06"		IV/IC	= 27° ♏ 52' 06"
XI	= 5° ♋ 23' 18"		V	= 5° ♑ 23' 18"
XII	= 7° ♌ 03' 52"		VI	= 7° ♒ 03' 52"
I/Asc	= 2° ♍ 30' 44"		VII/Desc	= 2° ♓ 30' 44"
II	= 26° ♍ 20' 37"		VIII	= 26° ♓ 20' 37"
III	= 23° ♎ 32' 46"		IX	= 23° ♈ 32' 46"

♊ and ♐ intercepted

2) January 14, 1935; ST = $10^h 33^m 14^s$; OE = 23.448889°;
geocentric latitude = 52.213013° **S**; RAMC = 158.30833°; MC = 156.559047°;
Asc = 280.61609°

    I.   OAHC

          OAXI = 188.30833°
          OAXII = 218.30833°
          OAII   = 278.30833°
          OAIII = 308.30833°

    II.   QHC

          QXI = QIII = 32.817909°
          QXII = QII = 48.163264°

    III.   Cusp longitudes

        XI

          A = 34.093631°
          COAXI = 253.75614°; OAXI < COAXI
          cusp = 192.51182°

        XII

          A = 26.900509°
          COAXII = 241.0203°; OAXII < COAXII
          cusp = 246.04618°

        II

          A = 130.17806°
          cusp = 300.24966°

        III

          A = 106.85244°
          cusp = 316.44589°

    IV.   Summary

X/MC	= 6° ♍ 33' 33"		IV/IC	= 6° ♓ 33' 33"
XI	= 12° ♎ 30' 43"		V	= 12° ♈ 30' 43"
XII	= 6° ♐ 02' 46"		VI	= 6° ♊ 02' 46"
I/Asc	= 10° ♑ 36' 58"		VII/Desc	= 10° ♋ 36' 58"
II	= 0° ♒ 14' 59"		VIII	= 0° ♌ 14' 59"
III	= 16° ♒ 26' 45"		IX	= 16° ♌ 26' 45"

                    ♉ and ♏ intercepted

3) July 12, 1978; ST = $12^h 22^m 38^s$; OE = 23.439444°;

geocentric latitude = 21.41829° **N**; RAMC = 185.65833° MC = 186.16349°;

Asc = 266.2291°

    I.   OAHC

$$OAXI = 215.65833°$$
$$OAXII = 245.65833°$$
$$OAII = 305.65833°$$
$$OAIII = 335.65833°$$

    II.   QHC

$$QXI = QIII = 11.096679°$$
$$QXII = QII = 18.763168°$$

    III.   Cusp longitudes

XI
$$A = 77.82912°$$
$$cusp = 215.81735°$$

XII
$$A = 98.04043°$$
$$cusp = 240.68322°$$

II
$$A = 59.024147°$$
$$COAII = 278.46954°;\ \ OAII > COAII$$
$$cusp = 296.19504°$$

III
$$A = 57.844039°$$
$$COAIII = 274.87799°;\ \ OAIII > COAIII$$
$$cusp = 331.46094°$$

    IV.   Summary

X/MC	= 6° ♎ 09' 49"		IV/IC	= 6° ♈ 09' 49"
XI	= 5° ♏ 49' 02"		V	= 5° ♉ 49' 02"
XII	= 0° ♐ 40' 60"		VI	= 0° ♊ 40' 60"
I/Asc	= 26° ♐ 13' 45"		VII/Desc	= 26° ♊ 13' 45"
II	= 26° ♑ 11' 42"		VIII	= 26° ♋ 11' 42"
III	= 1° ♓ 27' 39"		IX	= 1° ♍ 27' 39"

♌ and ♒ intercepted

4) November 23, 1918; ST = 22^{h}47^{m}07^s; OE = 23.450278°;
geocentric latitude = 40.092814° **S**; RAMC = 341.779167°;
MC = 340.260849°; Asc = 56.78703°

    I.   OAHC

$$OAXI = 11.779167°$$
$$OAXII = 41.779167°$$
$$OAII = 101.779167°$$
$$OAIII = 131.779167°$$

    II.   QHC

$$QXI = QIII = 22.82778°$$
$$QXII = QII = 36.094873°$$

    III.   Cusp longitudes

XI
$$A = 89.820058°$$
$$usp = 10.844945°$$

XII
$$A = 107.49787°$$
$$cusp = 34.366707°$$

II
$$A = 52.69126°$$
$$COAII = 108.43684°; \quad OAII < COAII$$
$$cusp = 83.977106°$$

III
$$A = 53.109135°$$
$$OAIII = 100.52079°; \quad OAIII > COAIII$$
$$cusp = 120.75369°$$

    IV.   Summary

X/MC	= 10° ♓ 15' 39"	IV/IC	= 10° ♍ 15' 39"
XI	= 10° ♈ 50' 42"	V	= 10° ♎ 50' 42"
XII	= 4° ♉ 22' 00"	VI	= 4° ♏ 22' 00"
I/Asc	= 26° ♉ 47' 13"	VII/Desc	= 26° ♏ 47' 13"
II	= 23° ♊ 58' 38"	VIII	= 23° ♐ 58' 38"
III	= 0° ♌ 45' 13"	IX	= 0° ♒ 45' 13"

♋ and ♑ intercepted

5) March 15, 1964; ST = $16^h 13^m 06^s$; OE = 23.44375°;
geocentric latitude = 72.740801° N; RAMC = 243.275°; MC = 245.2063°;
Asc = 44.282764°; ⇨Note lat > (90° - OE)

I. PCED's

PCED1 = 225.76196°
PCED2 = 314.23804°

RAMC falls within "twilight zone": special polar equations must be used.

II. OAHC

OAXI = 213.275°
OAXII = 183.275°
OAII = 123.275°
OAIII = 93.275°

III. QHC

QXI = QIII = 58.14448°
QXII = QII = 70.264688°; QXII and QII > (90° - OE)

IV. Cusp longitudes

XI
    A = 17.289352°
    COAXI = 225.74222°; OAXI < COAXI
    cusp = 256.99142°

XII
    A = 3.8979609°
    COAXII is undefined
    cusp = 343.5144°

II
    A = 20.401779°
    COAII is undefined
    cusp = 54.080673°

III
    A = 37.601288°
    COAIII = 134.25788°; OAIII < COAIII
    cusp = 59.719577°

V. Summary

X/MC	= 5° ♐ 12' 29"	IV/IC	= 5° ♊ 12' 29"
XI	= 16° ♐ 59' 29"	V	= 16° ♊ 59' 29"
XII	= 13° ♓ 30' 52"	VI	= 13° ♍ 30' 52"
I/Asc	= 14° ♉ 16' 58"	VII/Desc	= 14° ♏ 16' 58"
II	= 24° ♉ 04' 50"	VIII	= 24° ♏ 04' 50"
III	= 29° ♉ 43' 10"	IX	= 29° ♏ 43' 10"

♈, ♋, ♌, ♎, ♑ and ♒ intercepted

KOCH

Koch

Thus far this series of house systems analyses has dealt with methods the most modern of which is late medieval. This last system, the Birthplace system of Walter Koch, was devised in the mid-Twentieth Century. This method of house division is so named by its inventor because all cusp calculations directly incorporate the actual birthplace latitude; whereas, systems such as Campanus and Regiomontanus use "quasi-latitudes" which differ from one house cusp to the next. The mechanics of Koch resemble Alcabitius' model, while the calculations are precisely those of Ascendant computation.

Where Alcabitius traces the projected diurnal motion of the Ascendant degree of the ecliptic, Koch projects the diurnal arc of the Midheaven, from the time of its ascension (before the birth time) to the time of its setting. As the MC degree proceeds to stations at trisections of its eastern semi-arc, the ecliptic degrees on the eastern horizon mark successive house cusps (XI and XII). Similarly, from culmination to setting the MC degree's attainment of trisections of the western semi-arc marks the setting of successive house cusps (VIII and IX) at the western horizon.

As with other house systems, information on Koch/Birthplace as a portrayal of an underlying attitude or philosophy is lacking. While the editors of the Larousse **Encyclopedia of Astrology** cite only Koch's attempt to create a perfectly birthplace-specific method of house division, I feel there may be more at work in the subconscious of any creator/inventor. Use of the Midheaven as a primary determinant of intermediate house cusps implies that society and our place in it defines our experiential frame of reference. Also, focussing on a higher level of consciousness, one might say that our highest aspirations tell us what functions our experiences will serve. All this operating, of course, within the limits of an overall Plan, regardless of our consciousness of it.

At least one astrologer I know of, Al H. Morrison, cites transits to Koch's cusp III as being frequently indicative of vehicular accidents. Even if one prefers a different house system for general practice, this information might be worth knowing for rectification work.

❧ *Calculations* ❧

Deriving the equations necessary to compute Koch house cusps requires a more detailed description of the system's mechanics. To begin with, the diurnal arc of the MC is part of a parallel of declination, and it will need to be translated to the equator, a great circle from which we can measure out the arcs and angles of spherical triangles (*cf.* Alcabitius).

Begin with the MC degree on the eastern horizon (Figure 1a). When the MC has moved one-third of its semi-arc toward the meridian, the ecliptic degree at the eastern horizon is cusp XI (Figure 1b). At the two-thirds point of the MC's "morning" trek, the degree on the horizon is cusp XII (Figure 1c). Logically, when the MC lies on the meridian, its position at the birth time, the ecliptic degree on the eastern horizon is the Asc. Note that at the outset of the process, the MC degree marked at the horizon its own longitude, and that of cusp X. At the other end of the semi-arc, the Asc marks its own longitude and its own oblique ascension (see **Part One**, *Definitions*, p. 6). By computing the oblique ascension of the MC degree at the horizon, we can express the eastern diurnal semi-arc in terms of oblique ascension, thus translating an arc of a parallel of declination to a great circle, the equator, as was done with Alcabitius (pages 79 - 81).

Computation of the MC's oblique ascension requires preliminary determination of two additional parameters: declination of the MC degree (Figure 2), and its ascensional difference (Figure 3). (These elements are defined on pages 4 and 6, respectively, in *Definitions*.)

In triangle ABC of Figure 2b,

$B = OE$; $C = 90°$; a = right ascension; b = declination; and c = longitude

In a right spherical triangle,

$$\sin b = \sin c \times \sin B$$

Substituting,

$$\sin (decl) = \sin (long) \times \sin (OE)$$

Or, if one prefers to calculate the MC declination from the RAMC,

$$\tan b = \sin a \times \tan B$$

Substitutions yield

$$\tan (decl) = \sin (RA) \times \tan (OE)$$

Results of these equations will bear an algebraic sign: + (plus) for north declination, or − (minus) for south declination. This sign must be retained throughout the following computations.

The next step is the determination of the ascensional difference of the MC degree (Figure 3a).

In triangle ABC of Figure 3b,

B = co-latitude; $C = 90°$; a = ascensional difference (a.d.); and b = declination

In a right spherical triangle,

$$\sin a = \frac{\tan b}{\tan B}$$

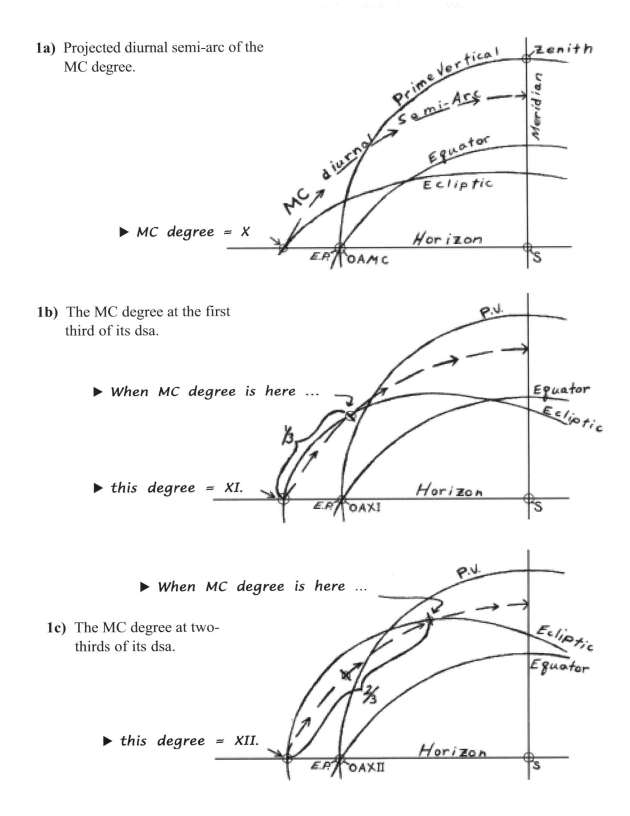

Figure 1: Koch Houses X, XI and XII

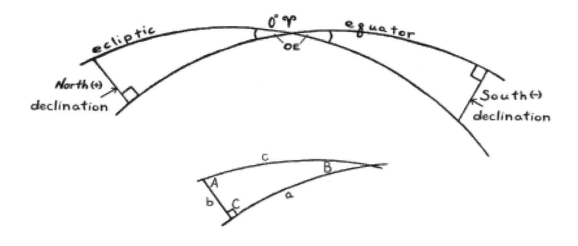

Figure 2: Declination

* * * * *

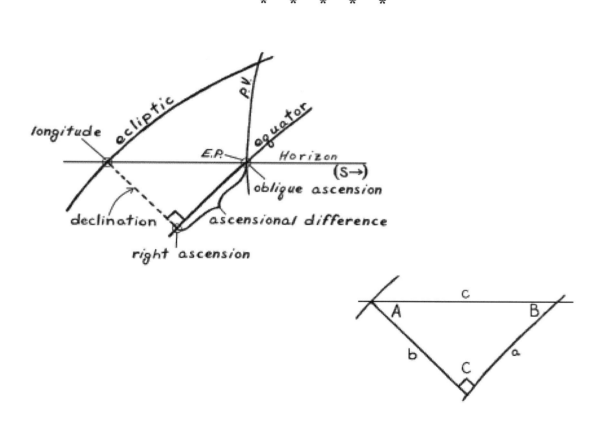

Figure 3: Ascensional Difference (showing north declination)

Substituting,

$$\sin(a.d.) = \frac{\tan(decl)}{\tan(co\text{-}lat)}$$

This statement can be simplified by substituting "latitude" for "co-latitude", its complement:

$$\sin(a.d.) = \tan(decl) \times \tan(lat)$$

Like declination, ascensional difference will be positive or negative, and its sign must be retained in the following calculations.

Ascensional difference is now used to calculate the oblique ascension of the MC at the eastern horizon:

$$OAMC = RAMC - a.d.$$

Note that

$$OAMC > RAMC \text{ for a negative a.d.}$$

$$OAMC < RAMC \text{ for a positive a.d.}$$

The third step is calculation of the eastern diurnal semi-arc (dsa) of the MC degree. Since both end points are now expressed in terms of oblique ascension for the given birth latitude, the required arc can be expressed as an equatorial arc by

$$dsa = OAAsc - OAMC$$

or, since $OAAsc = RAEP$,

$$dsa = RAEP - OAMC$$

The oblique ascension of house circles XI and XII is found by trisection of the diurnal semi-arc of the MC, with these one-third increments being added to the OAMC:

$$OAXI = OAMC + {}^{1}/_{3}\, dsa$$

$$OAXII = OAMC + {}^{2}/_{3}\, dsa \quad \underline{or} \quad OAXI + {}^{1}/_{3}\, dsa$$

The final step in cusp computation (for XI and XII) is the cusp longitude calculation. This is accomplished by use of equations for calculation of ascendants, each cusp being an ascending degree of the ecliptic. The only substitution of terms into the equations tabulated in "Asc Longitude Calculations" is "OAHC" (Oblique Ascension of House Circle) for "RAEP".

There now remains the calculation of cusps VIII and IX. The mechanical model provides this: when the MC degree has traversed the first third of its western diurnal semi-arc, the ecliptic degree on the western horizon is cusp VIII (Figure 4a). When the two-thirds station is attained, the ecliptic degree on the western horizon marks cusp IX (Figure 4b). Using the same type of analysis as for XI and XII, we can see that the end points of the western diurnal semi-arc, translated to the equator, are the oblique

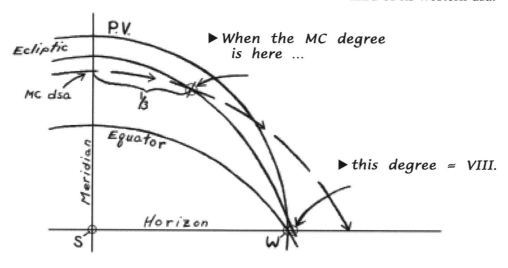

4a) The MC degree at the first third of its western dsa.

4b) The MC degree at the second third of its western dsa.

Figure 4: Koch Houses VIII and IX

descension of the MC (ODMC) and the oblique descension of the Descendant (ODDesc). Therefore

$$\text{western dsa} = \text{ODMC} - \text{ODDesc}$$

This obviously requires a new set of preliminary calculations for determination of oblique descension of various points; also, direct calculation of Descendants for a given hemisphere utilizes equations for Ascendants of the opposite hemisphere. However, this difficulty is overcome through a series of mathematical identities. The process will also permit the conventional practice of direct calculation of cusps II and III, rather than VIII and IX.

Begin with the logical progression of the MC degree past its two-thirds station (when IX is on the horizon): The MC "sets" at the western horizon, where its oblique descension is marked on the equator. As noted above, this corresponds to one end of an equatorial arc which began with the MC at the meridian and the Descendant on the western horizon. The other end of the arc is thus the ODDesc. This gives us the above equation for the western diurnal semi-arc. Now note that

$$\text{ODDesc} = \text{RAWP (RA of the West Point)} = \text{RAMC} - 90°$$

Also, trigonometric analysis along the lines of the OAMC computation will yield another useful identity:

$$\text{ODMC} = \text{RAMC} + a.d.$$

Making two substitutions into the original equation, we arrive at

$$\text{west dsa} = (\text{RAMC} + a.d.) - (\text{RAMC} - 90°)$$

$$\text{west dsa} = a.d. + 90° \quad \text{(remember to retain the algebraic sign of the a.d.)}$$

Now recall that

$$\text{OAAsc} = \text{RAEP} = \text{RAMC} + 90°$$

Therefore

$$\text{east dsa} = (\text{RAMC} + 90°) - (\text{RAMC} - a.d.)$$

$$\text{east dsa} = 90° + a.d.$$

Thus

$$\text{east dsa} = \text{west dsa}$$

The one-third dsa increments travelled by the MC degree east of the meridian are the same as those west of the meridian. This fact eliminates the need to calculate a western diurnal semi-arc. OAHC for cusps VIII and IX can be defined as

$$\text{OAIX} = \text{OAMC} - \tfrac{1}{3} \text{dsa}$$

$$\text{OAVIII} = \text{OAIX} - \tfrac{1}{3} \text{dsa}$$

However, since the motion of the MC by one-third its dsa causes all other points on the ecliptic and equator to move by that same angular distance, we can also say

$$OAII = RAEP + {}^1/_3 \, dsa$$

$$OAIII = OAII + {}^1/_3 \, dsa$$

Longitude of these houses is computed by using equations for ascendants, as for houses XI and XII.

❧ Southern Hemisphere ☙

Calculation of Koch houses for the southern hemisphere presents only one basic difference from northern hemisphere computations: lengths of diurnal arcs relative to the solstices. In north latitudes, diurnal semi-arcs exceed 90° for ecliptic degrees up to 90° either side of 0° ♋; either side of 0° ♑ the semi-arcs are less than 90°. The opposite is true for the southern hemisphere. The difference is resolved in the calculation of the OAMC, thus:

$$OAMC = RAMC + a.d. \text{ (regard being had for the sign of the a.d.)}$$

All other calculations follow the paradigm set for the northern latitudes. Equations for southern hemisphere ascendants are used in computing cusp longitudes.

❧ Circumpolar Regions ☙

Unlike other house division systems examined in this series, the Koch/Birthplace method cannot be used beyond the Arctic and Antarctic Circles for the following reasons:

1) Above a latitude equal to (90° - OE), there are certain ranges of sidereal times for which the ecliptic falls below the horizon (see *Arctic Region Asc Calculations*, p. 33). Should the MC degree fall within this range, which I have dubbed the "twilight zone", it will not ascend at the eastern horizon and will thus have no diurnal arc. No intermediate house cusps can be computed by Koch's method under these circumstances.

2) Since each cusp is calculated as an Ascendant, each house circle functions as a horizon with its own meridian and "quasi-RAMC". The latter is equal to (OAHC - 90°). If one or more of these quasi-RAMC's should fall within the twilight zone for the birth latitude, then successive intermediate house cusps may prove to be receding; *e.g.*, II may be 18° ♏ with III at 16° ♏, as is the case if the data in Example 5 below is used with an RAMC of 220°. Thus even if the MC of the birth chart be "in the clear", one or more of the house cusps will have a "quasi-RAMC" which is not. At best, the receding effect may not manifest in the "face values" on the cusps, but there will be some

point in the chart so calculated at which the ecliptic is, in effect, "folded" in so far as the math is concerned. (See p. 39 for more on the receding Ascendant.)

Points of failure for Koch can be defined thus:

1) Latitude > (90° - OE), north or south
2) Latitude = (90° - OE) N, ST = $18^h 00^m 00^s$
3) Latitude = (90° - OE) S, ST = $6^h 00^m 00^s$

❧ Summary ☙

I. Diurnal semi-arc
   A. MC declination
      1) MC decl = arcsin [sin (MC long) × sin (OE)]
      or
      2) MC decl = arctan [sin (RAMC) × tan (OE)]
   B. Ascensional difference
      a.d. = arcsin [tan (decl) × tan (lat)]
   C. Oblique Ascension of the MC
      1) North latitude: OAMC = RAMC - a.d.
      2) South latitude: OAMC = RAMC + a.d.
   D. Diurnal semi-arc (translated to equator)
      1) RAEP = RAMC + 90°
      2) dsa = RAEP - OAMC

II. Oblique Ascension of House Circles
   A. Trisect dsa
   B. OAHC

      OAXI = OAMC + ⅓ dsa
      OAXII = OAXI + ⅓ dsa
      OAII = RAEP + ⅓ dsa
      OAIII = OAII + ⅓ dsa

III. Cusps -- *Northern Hemisphere*
   A. 0° ≤ OAHC < 90°
      1) A = arccos [cos (OE) × sin (lat) +
         sin (OE) × cos (lat) × cos (OAHC)]
      2) COAHC = arccos [tan (OE) × tan (lat)]

145

3) Cusp longitude

    a. OAHC < COAHC

$$\text{cusp} = \arcsin\left[\frac{\cos(\text{lat}) \times \sin(\text{OAHC})}{\sin A}\right]$$

    b. OAHC = COAHC

    cusp = 90°

    c. OAHC > COAHC

$$\text{cusp} = 180° - \arcsin\left[\frac{\cos(\text{lat}) \times \sin(\text{OAHC})}{\sin A}\right]$$

B. 90° ≤ OAHC < 180°

1) A = arccos [- cos (OE) × sin (lat) -

        sin (OE) × cos (lat) × cos (OAHC)]

2) $\text{cusp} = 90° + \arccos\left[\dfrac{\cos(\text{lat}) \times \cos(\text{OAHC} - 90°)}{\sin A}\right]$

C. 180° ≤ OAHC < 270°

1) A = arccos [- cos (OE) × sin (lat) -

        sin (OE) × cos (lat) × cos (OAHC)]

2) $\text{cusp} = 180° + \arcsin\left[\dfrac{\cos(\text{lat}) \times \sin(\text{OAHC} - 180°)}{\sin A}\right]$

D. 270° ≤ OAHC < 360°/0°

1) A = arccos [cos (OE) × sin (lat) +

        sin (OE) × cos (lat) × cos (OAHC)]

2) COAHC = 360° - arccos [tan (OE) × tan (lat)]

3) Cusp longitude

    a. OAHC < COAHC

$$\text{cusp} = 270° - \arccos\left[\frac{\cos(\text{lat}) \times \cos(\text{OAHC} - 270°)}{\sin A}\right]$$

    b. OAHC = COAHC

    cusp = 270°

    c. OAHC > COAHC

$$\text{cusp} = 270° + \arccos\left[\frac{\cos(\text{lat}) \times \cos(\text{OAHC} - 270°)}{\sin A}\right]$$

IV. Cusps -- *Southern Hemisphere*

    A. $0° \leq \text{OAHC} < 90°$

        1) $A = \arccos [-\cos(OE) \times \sin(lat) + \sin(OE) \times \cos(lat) \times \cos(OAHC)]$

        2) $\text{cusp} = \arcsin \left[\dfrac{\cos(lat) \times \sin(OAHC)}{\sin A} \right]$

    B. $90° \leq \text{OAHC} < 180°$

        1) $A = \arccos [\cos(OE) \times \sin(lat) - \sin(OE) \times \cos(lat) \times \cos(OAHC)]$

        2) $\text{COAHC} = \arccos [-\tan(OE) \times \tan(lat)]$

        3)   Cusp longitude

            a.   OAHC < COAHC

$$\text{cusp} = 90° - \arccos \left[\dfrac{\cos(lat) \times \cos(OAHC - 90°)}{\sin A} \right]$$

            b.   OAHC = COAHC

                cusp = 90°

            c.   OAHC > COAHC

$$\text{cusp} = 90° + \arccos \left[\dfrac{\cos(lat) \times \cos(OAHC - 90°)}{\sin A} \right]$$

    C. $180° \leq \text{OAHC} < 270°$

        1) $A = \arccos [\cos(OE) \times \sin(lat) - \sin(OE) \times \cos(lat) \times \cos(OAHC)]$

        2) $\text{COAHC} = 360° - \arccos [-\tan(OE) \times \tan(lat)]$

        3)   Cusp longitude

            a.   OAHC < COAHC

$$\text{cusp} = 180° + \arcsin \left[\dfrac{\cos(lat) \times \sin(OAHC - 180°)}{\sin A} \right]$$

            b.   OAHC = COAHC

                cusp = 270°

            c.   OAHC > COAHC

$$\text{cusp} = 360° - \arcsin \left[\dfrac{\cos(lat) \times \sin(OAHC - 180°)}{\sin A} \right]$$

D. $270° \leq \text{OAHC} < 360°/0°$

1) $A = \arccos[-\cos(\text{OE}) \times \sin(\text{lat}) + \sin(\text{OE}) \times \cos(\text{lat}) \times \cos(\text{OAHC})]$

2) $\text{cusp} = 270° + \arccos\left[\dfrac{\cos(\text{lat}) \times \cos(\text{OAHC} - 270°)}{\sin A}\right]$

❧ Examples ❦

1) April 4, 1949; ST = $3^h\,42^m\,25^s$; OE = 23.448333°;
   geocentric latitude = 39.560115° N; RAMC = 55.604167°; MC = 57.868217°;
   Asc = 152.5121°

   I. Diurnal semi-arc
       A. MCdecl = 19.692441° (N)
       B. a.d. = 17.19734°
       C. OAMC = 38.406827°
       D. dsa = 107.19734°

   II. OAHC
       A. $^1/_3$ dsa = 35.732448°
       B. OAHC
           OAXI = 74.139275°
           OAXII = 109.87172°
           OAII = 181.33662°
           OAIII = 217.06907°

   III. Cusp longitudes
        XI
            A = 48.076641°
            COAXI = 69.003366°; OAXI > COAXI
            cusp = 94.635376°
        XII
            A = 118.68628°
            cusp = 124.25976°
        II
            A = 106.11676°
            cusp = 181.0726°
        III
            A = 109.847°
            cusp = 209.60787°

   IV. Summary

X/MC	= 27° ♉ 52' 06"		IV/IC	= 27° ♏ 52' 06"
XI	= 4° ♋ 38' 07"		V	= 4° ♑ 38' 07"
XII	= 4° ♌ 15' 35"		VI	= 4° ♒ 15' 35"
I/Asc	= 2° ♍ 30' 44"		VII/Desc	= 2° ♓ 30' 44"
II	= 1° ♎ 04' 21"		VIII	= 1° ♈ 04' 21"
III	= 29° ♎ 36' 28"		IX	= 29° ♈ 36' 28"

       ♊ and ♐ intercepted

2) January 14, 1935; ST = $10^h 33^m 14^s$; OE = 23.448889°;
geocentric latitude = 52.213013° **S**; RAMC = 158.30833°; MC = 156.559047°;
Asc = 280.61609°

    I.   Diurnal semi-arc
- A.   MCdecl = 9.1081413° (N)
- B.   a.d. = 11.933718°
- C.   OAMC = 170.24205°
- D.   dsa = 78.066282°

    II.   OAHC
- A. $\frac{1}{3}$ dsa = 26.022094°
- B.   OAHC
  - OAXI = 196.26414°
  - OAXII = 222.28624°
  - OAII = 274.33043°
  - OAIII = 300.35252°

    III. Cusp longitudes

      XI
- A = 16.444649°
- COAXI = 235.98208°; OAXI < COAXI
- cusp = 217.31412°

      XII
- A = 25.121885°
- COAXII = 235.98208°; OAXII < COAXII
- cusp = 256.18529°

      II
- A = 134.96036°
- cusp = 300.29306°

      III
- A = 127.00033°
- cusp = 318.5428°

    IV. Summary

X/MC = 6° ♍ 33' 33"	IV/IC = 6° ♓ 33' 33"
XI = 7° ♏ 18' 51"	V = 7° ♉ 18' 51"
XII = 16° ♐ 11' 07"	VI = 16° ♊ 11' 07"
I/Asc = 10° ♑ 36' 58"	VII/Desc = 10° ♋ 36' 58"
II = 0° ♒ 17' 35"	VIII = 0° ♌ 17' 35"
III = 18° ♒ 32' 34"	IX = 18° ♌ 32' 34"

♈ and ♎ intercepted

3) July 12, 1978; ST = $12^h 22^m 38^s$; OE = 23.439444°;
geocentric latitude = 21.41829°N; RAMC = 185.65833° MC = 186.16349°;
Asc = 266.2291°

    I.   Diurnal semi-arc
        A.   MCdecl = − 2.4477293° (S)
        B.   a.d. = − 0.9607857°
        C.   OAMC = 186.61912°
        D.   dsa = 89.039214°

    II.   OAHC
        A. $^1/_3$ dsa = 29.679738°
        B.   OAHC
            OAXI = 216.29886°
            OAXII = 245.9786°
            OAII = 305.33807°
            OAIII = 335.01781°

    III.   Cusp longitudes
        XI
            A = 92.097127°
            cusp = 213.4688°
        XII
            A = 100.62008°
            cusp = 239.89788°
        II
            A = 56.686027°
            COAII = 279.7918°; OAII > COAII
            cusp = 294.66703°
        III
            A = 47.878697°
            COAIII = 279.7918°; OAIII > COAIII
            cusp = 327.98957°

    IV.   Summary

X/MC	= 6° ♎ 09' 49"	IV/IC	= 6° ♈ 09' 49"
XI	= 3° ♏ 28' 08"	V	= 3° ♉ 28' 08"
XII	= 29° ♏ 53' 52"	VI	= 29° ♉ 53' 52"
I/Asc	= 26° ♐ 13' 45"	VII/Desc	= 26° ♊ 13' 45"
II	= 24° ♑ 40' 01"	VIII	= 24° ♋ 40' 01"
III	= 27° ♒ 59' 23"	IX	= 27° ♌ 59' 23"

♍ and ♓ intercepted

4) November 23, 1918; ST = $22^h 47^m 07^s$; OE = 23.450278°;
geocentric latitude = 40.092814° **S**; RAMC = 341.779167°;
MC = 340.260849°; Asc = 56.78703°

    I.   Diurnal semi-arc

        A.   MCdecl = - 7.7241616° (S)
        B.   a.d. = - 6.5566761°
        C.   OAMC = 335.22249°
        D   dsa = 96.556673°

    II.   OAHC

        A. $^1/_3$ dsa = 32.185558°

        B.   OAHC

            OAXI = 7.4080477°
            OAXII = 39.593605°
            OAII = 103.96472°
            OAIII = 136.15028°

    III.   Cusp longitudes

        XI
            A = 106.79456°
            cusp = 5.9136789°

        XII
            A = 110.86958°
            cusp = 31.452946°

        II
            A = 48.371178°
            COAII = 111.41893°; OAII < COAII
            cusp = 83.385563°

        III
            A = 35.866843°
            COAIII = 111.41893°; OAIII > COAIII
            cusp = 115.23933°

    IV.   Summary

X/MC = 10° ♓ 15' 39"		IV/IC = 10° ♍ 15' 39"	
XI = 5° ♈ 54' 49"		V = 5° ♎ 54' 49"	
XII = 1° ♉ 27' 11"		VI = 1° ♏ 27' 11"	
I/Asc = 26° ♉ 47' 13"		VII/Desc = 26° ♏ 47' 13"	
II = 23° ♊ 23' 08"		VIII = 23° ♐ 23' 08"	
III = 25° ♋ 14' 22"		IX = 25° ♑ 14' 22"	

♌ and ♒ intercepted

5) March 15, 1964; ST = $16^h\,13^m\,06^s$; OE = 23.44375°;
geocentric latitude = 72.740801° **N**; RAMC = 243.275°; MC = 245.2063°;
Asc = 44.282764°; ⇨ Note lat > (90° - OE)

Since the birth latitude exceeds (90° - OE), Koch houses cannot be computed for this birth data.

Diagrams and Models

The diagrams presented here are an attempt to push a spherical surface onto a flat plane in order to depict the interactions of the geodetic great circles (meridian, horizon and prime vertical) with celestial circles (equator and ecliptic). However, flat drawings do not always clearly convey the spatial configurations involved. I found a useful physical model for clarifying and verifying the trigonometric models presented in this manual to be a home-made armillary sphere. This tool is a physical representation of the various great circles and their interrelationships.

The instrument I have used was made as follows: First, I "borrowed" from my sons a nearly deflated whitish play ball (it looks more like Jupiter) and cut small holes at carefully located poles. Next I filled it with a moderate amount of spray urethane foam insulation (probably unhealthy stuff) purchased from a hardware store, to give the ball some solidity (a little of the stuff goes a long way!). A quarter-inch dowel serves as an axis, thrust through the filling while soft. The lower end of the polar axis is stuck in a hole drilled into a wood block at about 23° from the vertical.

I next made a small table from mat board with a circular cut-out slightly larger than the ball. The height of the table is just to the middle of the ball. Around the hole is marked the ecliptic longitude, going counter-clockwise as viewed from above.

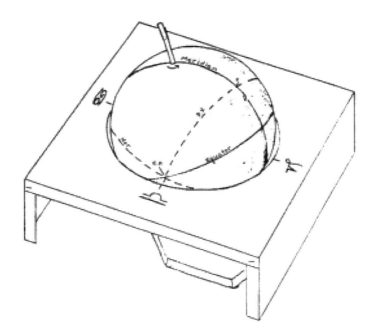

Permanently marked on the ball are an equator and a meridian, the latter having a few hash marks at estimated latitudes. If the table is of appropriate height, the equator will intersect the ecliptic plane at points just 180° apart. Orient the ball and its stand to the table so that the equator crosses the ecliptic at ♈ and ♎, rising above ♑. With wipe-off crayons I draw in prime verticals, horizons, house circles, etc. Turning the ball counter-clockwise in its table simulates the earth's rotation. Align the meridian with any given MC by rotating the ball, and the horizon for the chosen latitude will cross the ecliptic table at the Ascendant and Descendant. Note how a point on the ecliptic might appear against the horizon from the surface of the ball, and diurnal arcs and semi-arcs can be envisioned. Play and observe!

Quite possibly a globe would stand substitute for the ball, but I would hesitate to draw on one. I suppose "armillary sphere" is not the proper name for this facsimile of the medieval implement, not being made from *armillae*, but the function is the same, and I lack a better name. The instrument may want somewhat in precision, but it makes up for that in its ability to depict clearly the changing aspect of the ecliptic with regard to the mundane great circles as the earth rotates.

Made in the USA
Middletown, DE
22 March 2015